Collegiality and Bureaucracy in the Modern University

*The Influence of Information and Power
on Decision-Making Structures*

James L. Bess

**TEACHERS
COLLEGE
PRESS**

*Teachers College, Columbia University
New York and London*

For Nancy

Published by Teachers College Press, 1234 Amsterdam Avenue,
New York, NY 10027

Library of Congress Cataloging-in-Publication Data

Bess, James L.
  Collegiality and bureaucracy in the modern university.

  Bibliography: p.
  Includes index.
    1. Universities and colleges — United States —
Administration.   2. Organization.   3. Decision-making.
I. Title.
LB2328.2.B47   1988   378.73   87-18004

ISBN 0-8077-2868-3

Manufactured in the United States of America

92 91 90 89 88   1 2 3 4 5 6

CONTENTS

PREFACE

The chapters comprising this book represent somewhat independent and self-contained arguments, often quite speculative, and certainly without empirical backing. They are "loosely coupled," to borrow a well-known phrase. My aim can be construed as quite selfish. I wish to clarify my own thinking about the nature of the decision-making structure and process in colleges and universities. Toward that end, for the last five years, I have been carefully working my way through a variety of literatures that may bear on the subject. I have identified several promising conceptualizations, each of which offers insights into this domain, but none of which explains it all. This book, then, represents my current appraisal of the utility of various theories, with only a modicum of effort addressed to integrating them into a "grand theory" that will help decipher the complexities of this most interesting phenomenon.

The reader will immediately observe that I have omitted discussion of several critical thinkers, some of whose theories are clearly relevant to higher education. This is partly because I have set some constraints on the agenda for this book. In particular, I have chosen not to discuss in any depth the key elements in so-called "contingency theory" today — namely, environment, technology, and size. My sense is that these are crucial to understanding the basic structure of university organization, especially as contemporary "critical theorists" conceive of these variables. Most of the leadership in higher education makes assumptions about these contingencies that are unexamined, empirically unproven, and ideologically biased. The result is an organizational design that is often seriously flawed, as I have noted in previous writing on this subject (Bess, 1982).

In this book, however, I have begun with the typical university organization as it presently exists, not as it might be. I take as a given the organizational structures that we find in higher education and try to understand and explain their presence. As the reader will note, the central ideas employed in this effort are information flow, needs for coordination, power, and collegiality. My hope was to explore alternative conceptualizations of these notions and to see how they may help to unravel the complex mysteries of university organization.

As noted above, the chapters can be read independently and are for the most part self-contained. Some will find the language to be too abstract; others, too simplistic; and still others, naive. I write with two audiences in mind. The first is the higher education community, whose exposure to literature in organizational theory is for the most part quite limited. Hence, I have erred, perhaps, on the side of overexplanation of key ideas. The second is the "organizational behavior" fraternity, for whom higher education as a field of study is now becoming more legitimate. My intent in their regard is not to create new theory (though there may be some small increments on occasion) but to demonstrate how promising present theory may be in application in this field.

This, then, is really a work in progress. I acknowledge the hubris that is reflected in my belief that what I have to say is worth attending to, even if unfinished. On the other hand, it takes some immodesty, if not self-deception, to claim that a work is finished! One of Picasso's wives, Jacqueline, urged him continually not to hang his paintings on the walls of their house because she would almost invariable find him there weeks later tinkering with them — ever unsatisfied. These chapters have helped me learn. They constitute for me what Dewey called "an experience" — a completed whole from which I can hopefully move to higher levels of integration.

To those who would criticize the abstract nature of this effort by recalling William James' caution ("concepts without percepts are empty; percepts without concepts are blind"), I would respond with a story told to me by a wise philosophy professor in graduate school. Socrates, in Plato's *Republic*, he reminded the class, travels a complicated and ambitious intellectual path as he pursues his quest for an understanding of the nature of the human community. He moves steadfastly upward toward more abstract and theoretical musings on the meanings of life. He is also described as making a physical journey — from the agora, or marketplace, in Athens, with its palpable sights and sounds and pungent smells of barter, to the higher mountainous elevations, with clean, pure air and quiet atmosphere. His students, however, pull on his toga as he climbs, urging him to return to the "real" world. Socrates knew better. It is ever more pleasant to contemplate in the heights. But there is, after all, work to be done, and I hope that others will bring the thinking of this book home to the academic marketplace, where it will be of some use.

ACKNOWLEDGMENTS

Kind enough to labor through early drafts of this book were good friends and colleagues whose sharp intellects gave me no quarter. Would that I had listened more to Harland Bloland, Robert Silverman, Oscar Chase, Martin Finkelstein, Daniel Griffiths, and James Hoyt, but I must confess to insisting too stubbornly on retaining whatever sloppy or slippery thinking the reader may discover. Finishing touches on the book applied during my sabbatical were made easier through the accommodations afforded by the National Institute for Educational Research in Tokyo, especially with the help of Tatsuo Yamada. And a kind word must go to my computer/word processing guru, Edward Bracha, at St. Joseph's International School in Yokohama, who patiently facilitated and endured my many visits to his computer center. Cynthia Frank, a graduate assistant at New York University, must also be thanked for attending faithfully and promptly to my frenetic overseas requests for bibliographic assistance.

The business of making a book out of author hunches and scribbles was ably and tactfully performed by Teachers College Press, most skillfully by Audrey Kingstrom, whose insistence on yet another rewriting tested my author vanity but in the end served me well. The Press' Sonia DiVittorio and her staff intelligently and deftly untwisted my garbled meanings in their highly professional editing.

Finally, I owe much to my family for insights on organizations. How better to learn about power in clans than by living with two sons, one who is a teenager, the other who thinks he is; and about collegiality and trust, when one's wife espouses and lives those norms always. I thank them all.

Introduction

Organizational Problems of Colleges and Universities

The history of higher education has attracted its fair share of attention from scholars in recent years. Institutional and general histories now routinely document major shifts in purpose and/or structure. Among the particularly salient trends noted are the origins of colonial colleges as schools of theology, the rise of denominational colleges as missionary institutions in the early nineteenth century, the postbellum expansion of institutional purpose to include research and service (in the few colleges that were the forerunners of the modern university), and the emergence of the diverse complex of public and private colleges and universities that now constitute higher education.

As the nation changed in economic structure, demography, and values, so also did the roles of education. Changing demands on educational institutions forced corresponding shifts in goals and objectives and the ways of achieving them. Further, with the acceleration of the production of new knowledge and the concomitant rise in the professionalism of teachers and researchers came new perspectives on who should shape and control education. The tradition of lay control in the elementary and secondary levels, still a strong force in most communities today, gave way gradually in higher education to a more laissez-faire attitude. The public became increasingly

1

unable and reluctant to interfere directly with the management of colleges and universities, much as they feared to question the wisdom of professionals in other fields. On the other hand, government agencies and corporate enterprises exerted indirect influences through investments in human resource development and research productivity. And, of course, boards of trustees, though often self-perpetuating, were at least partially receptive to public concerns for responsible fiduciary management. Indeed, in public higher education, the pendulum of control has returned to the right, with often severe constraints placed by central bureaucracies on the very substance of academic affairs.

These various forces—autonomy, multiple missions, varied technologies, professional staffing, and new sources of funding and influence—have led to what is certainly one of the least understood forms of organization in the modern world—the contemporary college and university. Though the characterization by Cohen and March (1974) of universities as "anarchic" overstates the real condition (see Chapter 1), it does reflect the confusion in the literature about the forces that determine how colleges and universities are organized and administered.

Theories of Organization and Administration

Three of the four prevailing theories of organization and administration of colleges and universities are the well-known bureaucratic, collegial, and political (Baldridge, Curtis, Ecker, & Riley, 1978). The fourth is the "organized anarchy" of Cohen and March (1974). The first three correspond roughly to three long-standing and competing theories of (or, at least, "perspectives" on) organization found in a literature too infrequently invoked in the study of higher education—industrial and organizational psychology. These are: bureaucracy, human relations, and conflict. Each of these perspectives is based on and shaped by underlying assumptions about human nature, social systems, and the strength of contingencies that drive and constrain organizations.

The bureaucratic model is basically the mechanistic one, grounded in the observations of Weber (1947) and extended in the principles of scientific management. The guiding principle here is that human beings can be programmed in the same way as machines through a careful analysis and planning of job design and organizational structure. Moreover, workers will be content in positions in which they see themselves as legitimately placed by virtue of expertise and career. The processes of decision making in this model are decentralized to persons at the lowest possible organizational levels appropriate to the type of decision, with recourse to persons in positions at upper levels when insufficient expertise exists below. Conflict is presumed to be temporary and resolvable through the acknowledged, legitimate hierarchy.

The collegial model[1] (Millett, 1962, 1978) borrows the assumptions of the "human relations" or "human resources" school (Miles, 1965). The model places the individual above the organization in terms of priority of attention. Writers in this school (in contrast, some would say, to the one above) would insist that "inducements" must be offered to individuals to participate fully and be committed to the achievement of organizational ends. These investments must be designed with personal developmental needs weighted as heavily as the attainment of organizational ends. Only then will the *quid pro quo* in "contributions" be forthcoming (March & Simon, 1958).

A latent assumption of this school is that participation in decision making answers some fundamental universal need for feelings of control, or at least partial control, over one's work. Collegial forms of organization, then, describe patterns of "shared authority" (Mortimer & McConnell, 1978) in which those affected by decisions are deemed legitimately to have rights of participation. The nature and amount of the participation are commonly perceived ambiguously in most academic organizations and as varying in "administrative dominance," "administrative primacy," "faculty dominance," "faculty primacy," or "shared authority" (Mortimer & McConnell, 1978, p. 11; Kenen & Kenen, 1978). Presumably, a perfectly designed collegial system would permit members of the institution to participate in all matters that they felt were relevant to their personal needs, regardless of the organizational legitimacy or need for that participation.

The structures of decision making under the collegial model appear, therefore, to be rather cumbersome, redundant, and inefficient, as participation tends to be fluid and permissive, rather than constrained by organizational needs. Decision-making processes in collegial organizations also tend to be more discursive, rather than parsimonious, as all interested parties must be given opportunities to have their say, both formally and informally. Note that in the bureaucratic model, organizational ends predominate. Workers ac-

---

1. The "governance" or decision-making connotations of the model are referred to here. In Chapter 6, this conception is expanded.

cede quite readily to inclusion in or exclusion from decision making on the assumption that a rationally designed organization also attends to their needs. In both models, organizational image and anticipatory socialization play important parts in predisposing organizational members to expect to participate in varying degrees (Bess, 1978; Etzioni, 1961). As Baldridge et al. (1978, p. 33) note, the collegial model tends to be normative, rather than descriptive, and assumes that conflict is not functional and can be eliminated through consensus-oriented discussions. The model thus borrows heavily from the language and moral tone of the "organizational development" or "OD" literature.

Still a third model has arisen in recent years and appears to have been accepted by many observers in higher education as more valid than the previous two models. Among writers in the field of higher education, the model is called "political" and stems largely from the work of Victor Baldridge (1971). Its counterpart in the organizational theory literature is the conflict model, which is based on the notion of inevitable and irreconcilable differences among organizational participants. As Perrow (1973) notes, the political model downplays the notion of a "cooperative system" (Barnard, 1938), which normatively calls for a community of workers bound by efficient modes of communication about work matters. In the political model, the division of labor, endemic to complex organizations, constrains workers to displace goals and to "suboptimize" around subunits rather than the organization as a whole. Combined with accompanying breakdowns in communication that "limit their rationality," workers, proponents of this school suggest, will invariably find themselves in conflict with one another. The resolution of those conflicts, in turn, will take the form of bargaining and politics, in contrast to organizationally rational decision making under the bureaucratic model or consensus formation under the collegial. Decision-making structures in the political model can be either bureaucratic or collegial, or both, with politics as a process impinging on both. In contrast to the Baldridge et al. position and in accordance with the findings of Childers (1981), there is no universal decision-making structure for the political model. Rather, the political model can best describe the *processes* of decision making under assumptions of the conflict model found in the organizational literature.

The fourth and final salient model (though see the "matrix" model of Bess, 1982) is Cohen and March's (1974) "organized anarchy." The labeling of this approach as a "model" is perhaps inappropriate, as it is more a loosely connected set of propositions, occasionally with empirical backing, about both structure and process in organizations. The idea that organizations may be more or less anarchic seems to have arisen in response to the frustrations of many in the field of organizational behavior who were unable to establish with any reasonable degree of certainty cause and effect relationships among key structural or processual variables. This has led to the recognition that in many organizations, connections among organizational participants or units are "loosely coupled" (Weick, 1976) and that the culture of the organization — its norms, values, latent goals, hidden agendas, idiosyncratic characteristics — plays a far greater role than previously imagined (cf. Deal & Kennedy, 1982). Cohen and March (1974) have attempted most provocatively to describe this amorphous quality of organizational life.

In a related volume, March and Olsen (1976) suggest that observers of organizations tend to ignore aspects of decision making that are critical to understanding why decisions are (and, more importantly, are not) made. They note that organizational choices are encumbered by agendas other than the most obvious. Choice processes, they observe, are occasions for "executing standard operating procedures . . . , defining virtue and truth, distributing glory or blame . . . , expressing and discovering 'self-interest' and 'group-interest' . . . , [and] having a good time" (p. 12). The authors also suggest that choices in organizations are "fortuitous confluences" of problems, solutions, participants, and choice opportunities (p. 27). The fluid participation of organizational members in decision-making processes is somewhat constrained in the March and Olsen model by the nature of the structure of "participation rights." Thus, for some decisions, any decision maker can take part in the decision; for other decisions, hierarchical position in the organization sets the boundaries for participation; while for still others, the particular decision, rather than the structure, determines who will participate.

While the notions put forth by Cohen and March and others about the streams of problems and decisions in higher education have some merit in provoking new ways of thinking about both process and structure, such thinking tends to underestimate the more stable ongoing nature of college and university organization. There is a continuity and tradition on most campuses with respect to problem solving and decision making in most areas. The approach just outlined seems to treat each decision as unique, and while, to be sure, there are many unique decisions (some "created" as unique when they are truly routine), a large majority of decisions are han-

dled in accordance with well-accepted processes embedded in equally well-accepted structures.

On the other hand, what may occasionally be unclear and thus a
cause of conflict are the boundaries of participation in key decisions.
What Barnard called the "zone of indifference" to decision making
by authorities is clouded in higher education by the ambiguity of
authority rights, particularly when there are shifts in central leadership and leadership style or changes in the external environments of
higher education. Indeed, since relatively few important decisions at
the departmental level are needed in a typical academic year, and
since most faculty members are neither experienced nor skilled in
the routines of decision making, the perceptions of the process may
render the decisions organizationally nonroutine when indeed they
would be conceived as routine by most outside observers. As noted
in later chapters, there are also "political" reasons for faculty resistance to routinization of legitimately routine decisions.

The allocation of authority for decision making is subject to
many influences, of course. Whether a decision is viewed as routine
or nonroutine[2] is determined by the definition of the problem by
those in power. Whether a nonroutine decision is strategic or tactical[3]
depends importantly on the dynamics of the environment (Aldrich &
Pfeffer, 1976). Again, interpretation of the environment is a role
taken by the dominant coalition. As Mintzberg, Raisinghani, and
Theoret (1976) observe, strategic decisions involving the environment are based on perceptions of the quantity and shape of ambiguous data as well as action thresholds (behavior repertories) of the
organizational members (those thresholds are themselves subject to a
number of other influences).

The existence of so many alternative views of the organization of
colleges and universities prompted me to search for some synthesis
that could reconcile them. The perspectives outlined in the following
chapters represent the results of that search. As will be noted, the
emphasis is not so much on the individual decision maker as on the
organization as the unit of analysis. The concern here is not so much
with types of individuals and the bases for their decisions as with the

---

2. Nonroutine decisions involve unexpected problems and solutions not available from existing behavior repertories. See, for example, Perrow, 1972.

3. Strategic decisions involve the redirection of the organization toward new
goals and the reallocation of significant resources; tactical decisions demand only
minor reinterpretations of unusual stimuli to fit into available repertories or minor
changes in the repertories.

reasons why organizations such as colleges and universities seem to have developed the typical decision-making structures found on most campuses (and which appear to have been reasonably successful, to judge from the longevity of institutions of higher education compared with profit-making enterprises). The search for explanations in the literature of higher education leads almost invariably to conceptualizations of colleges and universities as unique, hence requiring analytic modes and hypotheses that could be applied only in this setting. A contrary notion is presented here: The analytic tools will be seen to borrow quite heavily from the standard repertory of concepts and theories in the organizational behavior literature. I propose, for example, in Part 1 of this book to explain both structure and processes of decision making in higher education as responsive to four forces—needs for efficient flows of information up and down the hierarchy, needs for coordination across parallel units in the organization, the strength of collegial norms, and needs of members of powerful groups to forward their special interests, often to the detriment of others. These forces are, in turn, products of the contingencies of environment, technology, and size.

The reader will recognize the primary debts in the chapters in Part 1 to such prominent thinkers in the literature as Helsabeck (1973), Kilmann (1977), Galbraith (1977), Van de Ven, Delbecq, and Koenig (1976), and especially Pfeffer (1978). In Chapter 5, I will also suggest that "collegiality" is not a mystical and romantic potion imbibed by academics to render their interactions both civil and altruistic, but a collection of ideologies, structures, and behaviors that can be explained through such concepts as culture, structure, interdependence, and anticipatory socialization—concepts well known in the current organizational behavior literature (cf. Deal & Kennedy, 1982; Mintzberg, 1979, 1983b; Zand, 1972).

Part 2 of the book moves away somewhat from the nomothetic perspective to the idiographic. In these chapters, the concern is with the explanation of power and authority, not as they are structured and used, but as they are perceived by faculty. More particularly, I explore the influences first of various organizational characteristics on the ways in which faculty evaluate the effectiveness of administrative leaders—for example, the classification of types of decisions that leaders make, the classification of types of college and university organizations in which leaders make those decisions, and the identification of phases or stages of organizational evolution that cause leaders to take different kinds of action and, in turn, cause faculty to view those actions on different grounds. The theories of Parsons

(1951), Pfeffer (1977), Cameron and Whetten (1981), and Bacharach and Lawler (1980) are important in these chapters.

In Chapter 9, I break down further the decision-making process by looking at the faculty not as a monolith, but as a disaggregated congeries of different types of individuals. Groups of faculty are identified with varying dispositions or preferences for types of decisions and decision makers. Here I borrow heavily from the theories of Kilmann and Herden (1976).

To reiterate the general theme of the book, I intend to consider the matter of decision making in higher education using the perspectives of theory developed largely in the study of organizational behavior in the industrial sector. I do not mean to imply that colleges and universities are not different from other kinds of organizations. Rather, I would hypothesize that much can be learned about higher education using the tools of analysis already developed elsewhere, especially by industrial and organizational psychologists. The chapters that follow incorporate a variety of theoretical perspectives toward that end.

Part One

Organizational Influences on Decision Making

CHAPTER ONE

Colleges and Universities as Organizations— A Framework for Analysis

Those who work in academic institutions find it helpful to believe that college and university employees, environments, supervisory relationships, timetables, and accountability are significantly different from those of the nonacademic sector. Doubtless they are correct in their impressions; otherwise colleges and universities would appear to have little to offer as places of employment that could not be found elsewhere. If academics (both faculty and staff) were misperceiving the situation, over a period of time any myth of uniqueness would be exposed; hence, there probably are, indeed, pleasantly unusual aspects of employment in academic institutions (as well as the usual share of unpleasantness).

Unfortunately, the claim of uniqueness has tended to dissuade many analysts of college and university organization—both researchers and practitioners—from using the scientific, conceptual tools that have been developed successfully to explain organizational phenomena in profit-making enterprises in the United States. The state of behavioral science in the field of organizational analysis has become quite sophisticated, and, despite the objections of many who decry its allegedly low explanatory power, organizational theory has been widely used. This is especially true at some of our largest industrial concerns, where theory-based knowledge of human behavior in organizations has helped shape many organizational designs and leadership practices.

Oddly, while most organizational theory has been developed by faculty within business schools and departments of applied psychology, not much knowledge has found its way into the very institutions that supported the research. The reasons are not complex. One, as noted above, is that there is some skepticism among academic leaders (and followers) that organizational theory has anything to say to the "unique" qualitative conditions of the organization in which they work. Another is that the typical upper management leader in academia has had no formal leadership training. He/she usually has been chosen for the leadership position precisely because of prior experience in line activities, which are diametrically opposed in psychological requirements to the needs of the position. As one commonly cited example, academic scientists who have succeeded in the laboratory and library by virtue of their willingness and disposition to spend long and lonely hours in their research efforts are hardly the types of persons who are likely to be adept at the profusion of interpersonal activities demanded of a busy dean or department chairman. Yet, they are usually chosen as much for their research success (or, more likely, their reputation), as their interpersonal skills.

Another reason that research findings have not been widely used in academia is the low interest of most researchers in translating their results into language that is meaningful and readily accessible to busy administrators. Indeed, the print medium, which is used to communicate research data, has been found to be far less effective than oral communication as a preferred means of learning by executives.

In this book, I hope to demonstrate the utility of organizational theory as a means of explaining how colleges and universities operate. I hope to show that although the structures and processes that currently exist in educational institutions may differ significantly from those in the private sector, they can be understood well through use of the same "concepts" and "theories" as are applied in the study of profit-making organizations. It should be stressed, however, that this approach differs importantly from that of Peter Blau (1973) in that I seek not to demonstrate a homology of structure between colleges and institutions in the profit-making sector. Rather, I hope to show that, as in all organizations, college and university structures undergo normal strain as they adapt to changing conditions.

More specifically, colleges and universities are constrained toward "pure" bureaucracy or "organizational rationality" in the interest of stabilizing the internal decision-making processes (cf. Scott, Mitchell, & Birnbaum, 1981, pp. 304–305), while at the same time they are pressured toward looser structures that are more readily responsive and adaptive to external conditions, particularly when the latter are turbulent (cf. Francis, Turk, & Willman, 1983).

Instead of viewing the organizational structures in colleges and universities as aberrant and unique adaptations to the special needs of academia, however, I prefer to think of them as standard accommodations to normal organizational conditions. For example, by applying contingency theory using such concepts as environment, technology, size, culture, and power—the same concepts used in analyzing other than academic institutions—the distribution and use of authority, both structurally and processually, can be reasonably well explained. This is not to say that the structures and processes that will be found are homologous to those in the nonprofit sector or some portions of it, but it is to claim that the concepts and theories are isomorphic.

More particularly, as I will show, the stress on any bureaucratic system originating in excessive needs for information and coordination results in modes of structural change that are quite common outside of academia. Indeed, what is called "governance" in academic circles is really a rather well-known and widely used form of participative decision making in many sectors of the business world. What I hope to do, finally, is to demythologize some of the decision-making structures and processes in higher education that have terminologies different from those in nonacademic settings. Removing these conceptual constraints will permit more revealing and useful diagnoses of the nature of academic and administrative structures in colleges and universities.

One further difference in this approach from that of Blau should be noted. Blau asserted that not only are colleges and universities homologous structurally with business concerns, but the effects of size and bureaucratization are not as deleterious to teaching and scholarship as would be imagined from traditional views of how bureaucracies affect workers. In this book, I take the position that colleges and universities depart in interesting and significant ways from bureaucratic forms and that it is this very departure from (rather than adherence to) bureaucracy that renders them more efficient. As I will show, however, the departure has heretofore been characterized as a uniquely academic adaptation. I hope to demonstrate that it is a rather straightforward, standard organizational response to internal and external contingencies.

Still another difference from the conventional research literature on college and university organization lies in the departure of the approach in this book from that of Cohen and March (1974) in their *Leadership and Ambiguity*. As noted in the Introduction, Cohen and March submit the argument that institutions of higher learning are essentially "anarchic," having problematic goals, unclear technology, and fluid member participation. In my view, this perspective is somewhat misleading in its overestimation of the ambiguity of college and university operation. It confuses individual short-term decisions about academic tasks with the longer-term, collective decisions about institutional strategy and tactics. In point of fact, the vast majority of *joint* decisions (i.e., not single-person decisions) in these institutions are made rather routinely. There is a well-established bureaucratic procedure for handling decisions—most of which have been *judged* to be routine (sometimes, of course, to suit organizational convenience and avoid recognizing exceptional problems). It is reasonable to hypothesize that there is no greater degree of "fluid participation" in higher education than in other organizations of similar *complexity*. I would submit that what Cohen and March perceive as anarchy is a combination of professionals' lack of interest in most organizational matters that are irrelevant to their central concerns and a self-interest in pursuing unique career orientations. (Here, I agree, in principle, with Mortimer & McConnell, 1978.)

The "apparent" anarchy can be explained further in part by referring to what Garrett Hardin (1968) calls "the tragedy of the commons." Under conditions of relative munificence or slack, no harm is done to the system as a whole by the unmanaged or undermanaged use of community property or resources by individuals, particularly when each person's interests are independent of the others. Hence, faculty have no need for or interest in institutional management when funds for teaching and research are readily available. On the other hand, when there are conditions of scarcity—or perceived scarcity (i.e., threats to the adequacy of resources for personal or professional use)—there is a corresponding need to become involved in the management of the system. (Cf. March & Simon, 1958, pp. 121–122, on changes in aspiration level accompanying changes in munificence.) Faculty, out of self-defense, enter the governance system.

The ongoing existence of a governance structure with little work of substance to do and the apparent disorder of a decision-making system with slack resources are responses to the cyclical nature of organizational stress. To describe the system as anarchic, however, misrepresents the reality. First of all, the term "anarchy" has a derogatory connotation, implying that the system has either abjured governance or has been ineffectual in installing it on a stable basis. The consequences for any anarchic system are thought to be negative. This is hardly the case in academia, where most allege that the looseness in the system is functional.

To return to Hardin's point, what is tragic (or, to be somewhat less dramatic, what is dysfunctional) is that the "commons" may be violated before the need for governance is fully recognized. Faculty or groups of faculty may overgraze the institutional pastures as they pursue their individual careers with the extraordinary autonomy normally accorded them. As I will show in later chapters, there is a lag in the organization's response to changes in various contingencies. In addition, the organization is continually under stress from coalitions to distribute the common welfare inequitably. In this case, the term "anarchy" may be suitable. But the inequality of the rewards does not suggest anarchy, only power differences.

Of course, self-interested exploitation of the system by individuals is viewed by the collectivity as neither moral nor functional — it distributes rewards inequitably and denies support for those deserving it. But, in some ways, the anarchic proclivities and tragedies of the commons are safeguarded by the *organizational* nature of the college or university. While in communities the infringement of individual liberties must be addressed "delicately" by municipal, state, or federal officials, lest constitutional rights be seen as violated, in formal organizations excesses of individual self-interested activities are controlled by an administration and/or governance mechanism perceived to be legitimately responsible for *total* institutional oversight. Faculty are both aware and wary of the need for external control and are (usually) properly self-restrained. The governance structures for institutions of higher education recognize the dangers of the tragedy of the commons by institutionalizing controlling mechanisms — not by leaving the system to anarchy.

It is necessary to turn at this point, therefore, to an examination of the components of those controlling mechanisms and to an examination of the university as an organization.

The University as a System

Let us look first at the university "systemically," to identify the range of problems and organizational solutions to those problems to which we will direct our attention. Taking the conceptual framework of Talcott Parsons (1951), it is possible to adopt his suggestion that there are four "functional prerequisites" that every social system must satisfy if it is to survive. These are adaptation, goal attainment, integration, and latency. Decisions in organizations can be seen, then, as necessarily attending to one or more of the prerequisites, as follows:

Adaptation — securing and distributing monetary and other resources (e.g., raw material and personnel) in an efficient
manner.

Goal setting and achievement — making salient the objectives and
products of the organization, to both outsiders and insiders,
through the process of transforming raw material into valued
outputs. Decisions here revolve around technology, product
or people processing, and marketing.

Integration — making it worthwhile for units in the organization to
collaborate with one another. Here, coordination of people
and departments requires decisions.

Latency — keeping people motivated, without tension and anxiety
and with a sense of continuity. Decisions involving organizational climate, esprit, and cohesiveness must be made.

To make these more meaningful in the context of higher education, several illustrations of decisions appropriate to each prerequisite may be given. For example, one may see the adaptation prerequisite as partially satisfied through the acquisition of external funds
for student scholarships. A goal-setting decision might involve a
curriculum revision designed to make graduates of the school more
marketable in the local economy, while an integration decision could
be illustrated by the decision of a school-wide committee to share
faculty resources. A latency decision in a university might be a
president's reassurances to a worried faculty that enrollments have
"bottomed out."[1]

It should be evident even from these few illustrations that a
variety of decisions are needed to satisfy each of the prerequisites. It
is important to understand also that the decisions composing each
functional prerequisite are made through a number of decision-
making "structures." Each structure evolves and is shaped to be responsive to the special needs of the prerequisite. The structure also is
influenced by the culture of the organization and by the needs of the
members who, through coalition formation, have managed to establish their power. For example, predominance of a culture highly
supportive of human need satisfaction will tend to emphasize the
gratificatory prerequisites — goal attainment and integration — and
will have a decision-making structure that is more egalitarian in
nature. On the other hand, a culture dominated by powerful coali-

---

1. An elaboration of these prerequisites appears in Chapter 8 in a discussion of
administrator responsibilities for each.

tions will tend to create structures that perpetuate that power (Hills & Mahoney, 1978). Thus, a belief by a powerful dean and his/her associates that students applying to the institution are quite homogeneous in learning styles and objectives and in career goals will result in a bureaucratic organization quite different from one that would follow under other assumptions and that might call for more individualized attention (cf. Perrow, 1970, p. 81).

The structures also follow from *assumptions* about contingencies in the environment external to the organization and from other assumptions about the technologies and work-flow interdependencies required for the transformation of raw material inputs into finished outputs. In colleges and universities (again, as in all organizations — Lawrence & Lorsch, 1967), organizational leaders assess the conditions in the external system that support the institution, and make a determination about their relative complexity and stability (Bess, 1982). They also examine the internal processes that constitute the daily business of higher education. The usual processes of transforming raw material into finished products include the technologies of teaching, research, and public service (the primary line activities requisite to the achievement of the goal-attainment prerequisite noted above). There are also a variety of staff or service operations or processes performed to facilitate goal attainment (these addressing the remaining three prerequisites — adaptation, integration, and latency). That faculty are at various times line and at other times staff (Etzioni, 1964) reflects the spread of their roles across the Parsonian prerequisites.

Thus, the ways in which the functional prerequisites are met are contingent on some conditions in the university's internal and external environments and on the power of some to convince others that the conditions prevail in one form or another.

If these four groups of decisions are basic to any organization's proper functioning, and there are structures that emerge to attend to them, what is the nature of those structures and what principles underlie the processes that generate, sustain, and change them? First, note that decisions falling into the two functional prerequisites that are cross boundary — adaptation and goal attainment — appear to be distributed quite differently from those that are primarily internal — integration and latency. In the cross-boundary group some tend to be decentralized both vertically and horizontally, while others are only partially so. For example, some adaptation decisions (e.g., textbook decisions) are yielded to faculty in line positions, while others (e.g., policy matters such as rules for tenure) are allocated to collectivities like faculty senates, and still others (e.g., the tenure decisions themselves) are shared among holders of positions in both the formal administrative hierarchy and the faculty organizations. Chapter 6 will consider in some detail the "settings" for these prerequisite decisions.

In the internal group—integration and latency—the decisions are also distributed variously (for different reasons). Some integration decisions, for example, are handled by faculty qua staff through a committee structure (as in the case of curriculum), while some latency decisions (e.g., concerning institutional esprit) are managed by bureaucratically appointed officers or, in the absence of interest or talent there, by charismatic leaders who emerge to fill the vacuum.

An explanation of how these functions are distributed requires a discussion of the nature of the organizational structures that exist in colleges and universities. A further word is necessary first by way of clarification about the use of the word "decisions." The reference throughout the book to organizational decisions should be taken to mean activities of a strategic (cf. Frederickson, 1984) as well "operating and administrative" nature (Mintzberg, 1979, p. 59). In the former instance, I will be addressing issues that profoundly affect either structure or culture (as these are defined below), particularly as they tend to be more contingent on external circumstances. In the latter case, I refer to decisions taken either routinely or somewhat automatically in the normal course of organizational events. In other words, it is important to understand decision making in colleges and universities as a response to institutional needs both for adaptiveness and for regularized processes for solving problems that typically occur in the short run.

Domains and Structures of Decision Making

It is necessary at this point to be somewhat more specific about the range and kinds of decisions that are usually made in university settings. By classifying their variety, we can then move more logically to an understanding of their distribution throughout the organization.

Viewed from a systems perspective, decisions in at least four areas are needed to satisfy the prerequisites noted earlier. In higher education, these decision domains are:

1. Inputs, which are of two kinds: (a) "enabling" inputs, which give the institution the resources to do its work; and (b) raw material inputs. In turn, there are two kinds of enabling in-puts—monetary resources from external funding and sales receipts, and personnel resources to be added to or to replace existing staff. In the case of the university, raw material inputs include students to be changed in some way and knowledge to be manipulated and synthesized. ("Signal" inputs, which rep-resent information that crosses organizational boundaries, fall into the feedback design area noted in [4] below.) Input deci-sions fall into the adaptation prerequisite.
2. Transformational processes, by both line (teaching, research, and service) and staff (administration) personnel employed in the transformation of raw material. These decisions are part of the adaptation and integration prerequisites, as choices must be made about how to distribute resources, about tech-nologies, and about organizational design.
3. Quality of the outputs (graduates, publications) that exit the system. Decisions here fall into the goal-attainment prerequi-site.
4. Design of the feedback information system that signals partic-ipants about needed changes. This is both an adaptation and a goal-attainment function.[2]

These decision domains are established and controlled through the design and manipulation of two intertwined organizational mechanisms that orient and/or direct workers toward the perfor-mance of their roles. These are the well-known structural and cultur-al dimensions. The first is the structure of formal roles and responsi-bilities as they are aggregated into formally articulated patterns of departments and, equally important, as those departments and roles are linked through coordination mechanisms. What is meant in this book by this formal or official "structure" is what Pugh, Hickson, and Hinings (1969) call "full" bureaucracy, which is essentially an operationalization of Weber's (1947) "ideal" types. For those authors, three dimensions constitute the main structural characteristics of work organizations:

---

2. Note that this categorization overlaps that of Helsabeck (1973, p. 4), which is discussed later. It is, however, more exhaustive. See also Childers (1981), whose empirical study of the reputed dispersion of authority considers ten discrete do-mains.

1. Structuring of activities — specialization of roles, standardization, formalization.
2. Concentration of authority — amount of centralized control.
3. Impersonality of procedures — the relative control of work through impersonal rules rather than direct face-to-face control.

"Full" bureaucratic structures can be understood, therefore, as (1) comprising persons who are linked formally into completely specified, standardized interdependencies; (2) positions arranged in a system of formal, hierarchical authority that purports to prescribe all organizational interactions; and (3) impersonal rules governing all behavior. The question arises as to the extent to which colleges and universities are full bureaucracies and, if they are not, the reasons for the deviation from "fullness." Again, if they are, indeed, full bureaucracies, then the "rules" of explanation in the profit sector apply homologously. Further, if they are not, but the deviations are standard, again known modes of explanation of organizational phenomena will hold.

Colleges and universities comprise multiple decision-making units. As is well known, the nonacademic side of academia tends to resemble a business enterprise and thus is commonly found to be closer to full bureaucracy in structure. For example, the usual administrative departments — admissions, business operations, institutional advancement, and planning — tend to be more tightly bureaucratic. The academic side has a more varied structure. While in most universities "formal" authority for curricular and personnel matters technically resides in the positions found in the hierarchical structure, such authority informally, and sometimes formally, is given over to the faculty. (The degree of vesting depends on the nature of the organization — the larger, the more complex, and/or the more prestigious, the more complete the vesting.)

Academic operations are, of course, complicated by the "extra-hierarchical" addition of the typical faculty senate and its elaborate committee structure. To varying degrees, curriculum and personnel matters are regulated by the faculty, with persons occupying the administrative hierarchy interceding only when there are jurisdictional battles that cannot be adjudicated by the faculty apparatus itself. The particular modes of intercession or coordination constitute one measure of the dispersion of authority, as will be elaborated on in later chapters.

In addition to the separated domains of responsibility and control in a college or university, there are numerous structural arrangements in which joint participation is the mode. By this I refer to various standing faculty–administration committees charged with oversight of executive policy, curriculum, graduate education, presidential fellowships, library, commencement, and other functions and facilities. In organizations that are more professionalized, the formal organizational design is more "loosely coupled" (Weick, 1976). Vertical interdependencies are intentionally reduced, thus requiring more decentralized control and often leaving more discretion to the emergent informal system, or culture, and its peer values. Importantly, both the formal (e.g., committee) and informal control domains are to some degree subject to the influence of the dominant coalition (Zaleznik, 1970; Hickson, Hinings, Lee, Schneck, & Pennings, 1971; Salancik & Pfeffer, 1977; Pfeffer, 1978; Miles & Snow, 1978; Kotter, 1978). Coalitions routinely attempt to make determinations that forward their interests. How they gain and maintain their influence will be addressed in later chapters.

To some extent, decisions about organizational structure are not continually salient concerns of the dominant coalition, despite the fact that they are antecedent and/or in a causal relationship to the other four decision domains.[3] Needed changes in formal structure are extremely difficult to identify (Hardy et al., 1984) as well as to orchestrate (Weick, 1969; Beer, 1980, p. 73; Pfeffer, 1982, p. 226; Meyer & Rowan, 1977). There are several reasons for this.

First, as contingency theorists have well argued (see Van de Ven & Drazin, 1985), there are at least three powerful forces that critically determine the design of organizations. These are size (Blau, 1973), technology (Perrow, 1970) and environment (Lawrence & Lorsch, 1967). The design imperatives dictated by these contingencies place limitations on the possibilities for variations in organizational structure if organizational effectiveness is to be sustained or enhanced. In higher education, for example, differences in degree of "paradigm development" (Bresser, 1984) among disciplines account for organizational uncertainties. Paradigm development is one side of the technology dimension in the Perrow framework; for example, manifesting a variance in the "number of exceptions" in raw material encountered. Knowledge and/or data used in research, for instance, may be more or less certain depending on the discipline.

---

3. From a Marxist perspective, of course, the parallel is in the dominance of structure and culture over all forms of social and economic life.

Another illustration of the limitations of coalitional influence lies in the conditions external to the system. The turbulence of the research environments outside of each discipline also contributes to uncertainties (Pfeffer, Salancik, & Leblebici, 1976; Beyer & Lodahl, 1976; March, 1976). Both technology and environment in higher education, as conceived by some power incumbents today, call strongly for an organizational structure that is decentralized, if not atomized, in order to be readily adaptive and "effective" in exploiting markets (although recent theorists — e.g., Chandler, 1977; Francis, Turk, & Willman, 1983 — have suggested that this excessive market orientation may be ineffective in the long run). On the other hand, other conceptions of technology and environment would point to more bureaucratic structures. In either interpretation, once in place the structure tends to endure, resisting revision that would follow from alternative perspectives.

In sum, the definition of the natures of the contingencies is critical to the organizational design that evolves (cf. Berger & Luckmann, 1966; Salaman, 1980). However, there are limitations to the amount of variation that can be introduced, given the actual contingencies that exist. As a result of these forces toward stasis, questions of formal authority tend to arise relatively infrequently in all organizations (though the more dramatic nature of conflict over authority tends to make such issues seem omnipresent). In higher education, as one illustration, during the student protest conditions of the late 1960s, there was a rise in concerns that control mechanisms over a number of domains of interest (e.g., the transformation processes of teaching) were being threatened and that changes in structure might be deleterious to the interests of the dominant coalition. More plainly, faculty with vested interests in traditional teaching assignments saw a threat in student demands for a more "relevant" curriculum.

Another reason for the difficulty of changing structure is that it is among the more static, long-standing characteristics of organizations. Along with culture (discussed below), it is a major source of institutional image and thus attracts personnel who see a particular organization as an opportunity for personal gain through the reward framework of the extant system, rather than through some anticipated alternative system. Still a third reason is the oft-cited "academic procession" (Riesman, 1956), which causes mimetic structuring and posturing for status. As Meyer and Rowan (1977) observe, this is not a common phenomenon in the profit-making sector.

Organizational Culture

A second form of organizational control is exercised by workers themselves through the "culture" of the organization (Deal & Kennedy, 1982; Wilkins & Ouchi, 1983; Schein, 1985; Frost, Moore, Louis, Lundberg, & Martin, 1985) — that is, the informal system of norms and attitudes, the climate of esprit and cohesiveness (or lack of it), and the institutionalization of value (Selznick, 1957; cf. Steele & Jenks, 1977; Harrison, 1972; Clark, 1972; Meyer & Rowan, 1977; Pfeffer, 1982, p. 239). This normative structure and its connection to formally stated organizational goals has long been recognized as important to organizational effectiveness. In Chapter 5 of this book, the impact of culture on the structure of organizational decision making in higher education is examined in some detail. Before discussing the nature of that impact, however, it is necessary to complete the description of the elements that constitute the structure itself and of the nature of dispersion of authority within the structure.

The Dispersion of Authority

The four decision domains noted above — inputs, transformations, outputs, and feedback — are qualitatively different in data, time frames, and required expertise. Each calls for a unique decision-making structure in order for the decisions to be made efficiently.[4] That is, each evokes a set of unique organizational substructures, norms, beliefs, and behaviors that are appropriate to the particular decision area and that (in an efficient organization) are complementary to and may overlap with sets serving other domains. For example, in the domain of inputs, a structure for decision making about the characteristics of students to be admitted to the institution emerges, as does a set of beliefs about student admissions policy. The admissions substructure tends to comprise small groups of individuals operating at first individually, then collectively on input data on student characteristics. Decision making on the output side — for example, who should graduate — is carried out in different ways, on

---

4. The four dimensions in the framework of Kilmann (1977) capture these differences reasonably well, as described below. See also Thompson and Tuden (1959).

the one hand by faculty who decide collectively on graduation requirements and, on the other, by recording officials who match courses and grades against those requirements.

There are several tasks that must be accomplished if we are to understand and explain the dispersion of authority for decision making in universities. The first is to conceptualize the decision-making ingredients — the table of periodic elements that constitute the decision domains in higher education. This has been done through the identification above of the four decision domains. Second, the structures for decision making that are used to make those decisions must be articulated. Third, an organizational "map" showing the dispersion of these decisions must be created. And last, there must be an explanation of the reasons for both the structures and the dispersion.

Two models from the literature are of potential use for this task. They are presented here and utilized in later chapters. The first is the model developed by Ralph Kilmann (1977), which conceptualizes and characterizes different kinds of decision-making structures according to the special functions that they are especially well qualified to serve. The second is the model developed by Helsabeck (1973), which provides parsimoniously (with two independent dimensions) an explanation of how those structures are distributed throughout various kinds of organizations in higher education. The Kilmann model is presented first.

Four basic organizational designs (or "structures") are proposed by Kilmann to describe the modes of decision making in organizations. Each design serves somewhat different social system functions, and different organizations emphasize one of the four over the others. The four designs are: operational design, problem-solving design, informal design, and strategic planning design. Kilmann suggests that

> these different designs deal with the different components of organizational effectiveness and how an organization may need to have more than one design to be truly effective. Briefly, the organization can obtain (1) internal efficiency, by designing a viable OPERATIONAL DESIGN (one that emphasizes specificity, control, optimal work flow, etc.); (2) internal effectiveness, by designing a viable INFORMAL SYSTEM (allowing members to communicate across formal channels to satisfy social and informational needs); (3) external efficiency, by designing a viable PROBLEM SOLVING DESIGN (to confront the problems posed by the organization's environment); (4) external effectiveness, by

Figure 1.1
Configurations
of Organizational Structure

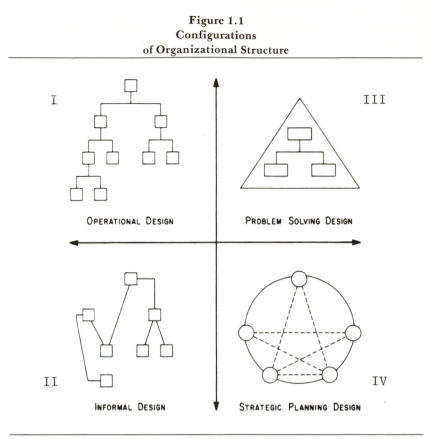

Reprinted with adaptations by permission of the publisher from Ralph H. Kilmann, *Social System Design: Normative Theory and the MAPS Design Technology*, p. 137. Copyright 1977 by Elsevier Science Publishing Co., Inc.

designing a viable STRATEGIC PLANNING DESIGN (to define the problems posed by the environment). (1977, p. 137)[5]

The four configurations of organizational structure are displayed in Figure 1.1.

---

5. Note the parallels to the Parsonian framework. Kilmann has, in effect, described the structures that are needed to meet each of the prerequisites. As discussed later, universities tend to concentrate on one prerequisite at a time (though not to the complete exclusion of the others), depending on the predilections of the dominant coalition. Hence, the decision-making structure in the Kilmann conceptualization will be modeled on those orientations.

One of the attractive features of this model is that it lends itself to an understanding of the influence of organizational culture on the allocation of decision-making authority to alternative structures that serve each of the four functions. Thus, a college with a strong concern for the maintenance of internal social relations might find authority vested more intensely in an "informal system" configuration, while a college with concerns for efficient operations (say, for example, in a period of decline) might move toward an "operational design" model. Interpretations of the concern often fall to coalitions that benefit from one or the other of the designs.

Of equal interest here is Kilmann's conceptualization both of the aims of each of the configurations and of the psychological dispositions of people who prefer them. As noted above, the primary aim of an organization in quadrant I in Figure 1.1 is internal efficiency (the minimizing of the ratio of inputs to outputs), and the organizational participants who most prefer this kind of organizational order are people who "approach effectiveness through detailed impersonal facts and impersonal analytical reasoning" (Kilmann, 1977, p. 182). Administrative personnel in most colleges and universities tend to match both the objectives and personalities of this description. On the other hand, the objectives of the structure in quadrant II are to maximize member motivation. Here we see the common "collegial" structure found at the departmental level or at smaller-sized colleges as a whole. Decision making in this sector tends to recognize the need to keep members satisfied and motivated.

The objective of the structure in quadrant III is to maximize the organization's bargaining position vis-à-vis the environment. This problem-solving structure describes the configurations typically established in the interface between faculty and administration. The concern is with more immediate problems—for example, eliminating overlapping courses, arranging for joint majors, and so forth. The structure also serves to describe the juncture between administrations and boards of trustees, where problems of ensuring continuity of resource inputs are managed.

The structure in quadrant IV is set up to address itself to longer-range issues of the relationship of the institution to society—problems of ensuring that the alleged ethical and educational goals of the institution are, indeed, being achieved and that society has properly benefited from the efforts of the participants of the institution. This particular structure best describes the typical institutional senate or plenary governance body. Persons aspiring to serve in these decision-making councils will, according to Kilmann's theory, be predisposed to seek facts and make evaluations "through the gestalt by synthesis and personalistic value judgments" (Kilmann, 1977, p. 182).

The Kilmann model will be used in later chapters to explain how and why authority for different types of problems is dispersed to one of the four quadrants. Inasmuch as there is some ambiguity over jurisdiction in problem solving in colleges and universities, we can understand the ultimate resolution of the authority question by conceiving of the alternative structural means of solving a problem as subject to a number of influences. For some kinds of universities, the dispersion of the problem to the most "efficient" quadrant will take place. For others, political considerations will cause the problem to be lodged in a quadrant that is not efficient in organizational terms and does not match the predispositions of the decision makers. In later chapters, the nature of these political versus collegial influences will be considered further. Here, however, the concern is simply with a map of the potential decision domains.

Having outlined the Kilmann model, it is now necessary to move to the second model noted earlier—that of Helsabeck (1973). This will permit the identification of a map on which the Kilmann structures can be placed.

According to the Helsabeck framework, one can describe the location of an authority structure in terms of two dimensions: centricity and participation. Centricity is the hierarchical level at which particular decisions are made, while participation reflects the degree of involvement of different organizational members in the decision making. The combination of these two dimensions permits the pinpointing not only of the particular location in the organization in which particular decisions take place, but also the mode of decision making in terms of numbers of persons involved (i.e., the sharing of authority).

The dimension of centricity runs from decisions made at a "corporate" level to decisions made in a federated mode. Participation extends from monarchic (i.e., single-person) decisions to "mass democratic." Crossing these dimensions results in the model noted in Figure 1.2.

Of particular value in this model is its capacity for depicting the confluence of academic and administrative decision making. Thus, for example, monarchic, federated decisions (quadrant IV) are recognizable as decisions made typically by department chairpersons alone (i.e., without input from either faculty or administration). Corporate, mass democratic decisions (quadrant I), on the other hand, are made at plenary sessions of the governing body, which

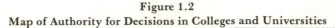

Figure 1.2
Map of Authority for Decisions in Colleges and Universities

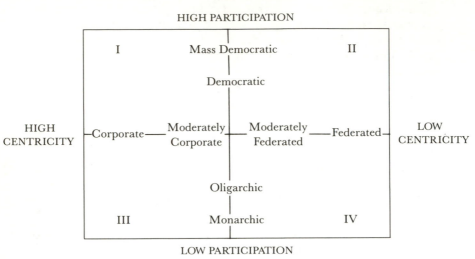

Adapted from Helsabeck (1973, p. 6).

comprises all members of the college or university community. Beyer and Lodahl (1976) implicitly used this framework in their comparative study of centralization and collegiality in British and American universities.

What is also useful about the model is its utility in allowing a display of the different decision structures as they may be arrayed throughout the four quadrants. Thus, it is possible that faculty appointment decisions might be made in a moderately federated, democratic way (quadrant II), while investment portfolio decisions might be made in a monarchic, corporate manner (quadrant III). The decision-making process can be characterized as a "compound system" (the name of Helsabeck's book). A variety of such compound systems is represented in the universe of colleges and universities, and by plotting the various authority structure locations of the different decisions for different types of institutions, one can get a sense of the shape of the authority structure for the complex of institutions across the country.

Helsabeck suggests further that there are four categories of decisions in higher education, the authority for each of which can be dispersed throughout an institution. They are: authority allocation, resource allocation, resource acquisition, and production.[6] In turn, each category of decision can be considered as having application to the system as a whole or to subsystems (e.g., to the university as a whole or some portion of it). Hence, there are eight possible types of decisions to be distributed.

Having thus described both the Kilmann and the Helsabeck models, it remains to combine them in order to maximize their explanatory utility. Figure 1.3 represents a superimposition of the Kilmann typology on that of Helsabeck.

It seems reasonable to believe that a tendency exists for organizations with structures aimed at maximizing internal efficiency to be more centralized and not to permit much member participation (though contingencies of technology and environment may vitiate this somewhat). Operational design and bureaucracy will thus often be found to overlap. Similarly, Kilmann's "informal design" structural configuration can be seen as fitting logically into the upper right-hand quadrant in the Helsabeck model—that is, as encouraging much participation on a decentralized basis (that mode being most likely to maximize member motivation). Academic department structures most commonly take on this shape.

Because of the multiple mission orientation of the typical university, structures designed with the intention of attending to problems in the environment (Kilmann, quadrant III) will most likely be found in more than one of the Helsabeck quadrants, depending on the decisions to be made (i.e., on which cross-boundary inputs or outputs are at issue). For example, one structure set up to handle this function will be found toward the midpoint of centricity in the Helsabeck diagram, as faculty and administration join in decision-making councils addressing these system-wide needs for mainte-

---

6. Note that the four categories differ somewhat from the functional prerequisites of Talcott Parsons described earlier and are not the same as the concepts in systems theory (inputs, transformations, outputs, and feedback). Since the Parsons framework appears more exhaustive (taking into account, for example, needs of the system for motivated employees), it will be used in discussions here as well as in later chapters. It also permits a clearer understanding of the independent variables that are responsible for the dispersion of authority (cf. n. 9, this chapter).

Figure 1.3
Matching of Structure Type and Authority Location

HIGH PARTICIPATION

Strategic Planning (KIV)	Problem Solving Design (1) (KIII)	Informal Design (KII)
HI		HII
HIII		HIV
Operational Design (KI)		Problem Solving Design (2) (KIII)

HIGH CENTRICITY

LOW CENTRICITY

LOW PARTICIPATION

Key: HI to HIV refers to Helsabeck quadrants
KI to KIV refers to Kilmann quadrants

Adapted from Helsabeck (1973) and Kilmann (1977).

nance of input stability. On the other hand, sensitivity to shifting environmental demands for research outputs requires decentralization (cf. Weick, 1978), as faculty personally or through their departments span organizational boundaries in their search for promising arenas of action. Hence, one might expect to find the problem-solving design in Kilmann's quadrant III in at least two of the Helsabeck quadrants.

Of interest is Kilmann's notion that different personality types will occupy (or at least prefer to occupy) these different decision-making structures. Kilmann's theory thus might lead to a prediction that faculty seeking research grants and opportunities may be quite similar in personality to personnel in institutional planning offices, thereby explaining the common decision-making structure but the different placement in the Helsabeck model.[7] (In Chapters 8 and 9, discussion of the impact of different personalities of leaders on faculty perception of their effectiveness extends Kilmann's ideas still further.)

Finally, it is logical to believe that strategic planning design (Kilmann, quadrant IV) will accurately capture the organizational characteristics of the typical university senate, where issues of meanings and impacts of higher education are discussed. Thus, this structure will be found in Helsabeck's quadrant I — more centralized, with heavy participation.

Dispersion Rationale

Having laid out these two models and shown their relationships, it is possible now to move to a discussion of the rationale for the allocation of particular types of decisions to one or more of the structures. Recall that both Parsons and Kilmann indicate that all four functional prerequisites must be addressed and all four objectives of the structures must be met, at least partially. The central question, then, for students of college and university organization is how and why authority over these four sets of functional or system decisions is allocated to different persons or bodies, either formally (structurally) or informally.

As noted above, some would insist that "governance" is a system of formal decision making that is *sui generis* to colleges and universities, largely because of the unique nature of faculty (especially their strong and traditional needs for academic freedom, combined with their status as professionals). In this book, the argument is made that while governance in higher education takes unusual forms, these forms can be explained parsimoniously using relatively few conceptual frameworks already in the extant organizational theory literature. In particular, in the chapters in this part of the book, the notions of information flow, coordination, and power are introduced as they serve to explicate the nature of higher education organiza-

---

7. Note that the Kilmann model assumes that organizational structures "fit" the personalities of the occupants of the structures and that the structures "fit" the needs of the system. He does not, nor is it the intention here to suggest that the forces of personality are a determinant of particular organizational structures, though it could certainly be argued that the leader of the dominant coalition might well have a strong influence.

tion. In Part 2, explanations from the literature on organizational culture are considered.

Several themes or theses guide the arguments that constitute the chapters in this part. The first is that the special needs of colleges and universities for decision making create flows of information that cannot be efficiently managed through traditional hierarchical forms of organization. The Weberian presumption that in an ideal bureaucracy knowledge and expertise are perfectly correlated is violated in higher education. Deans and vice presidents cannot possess adequate knowledge of all disciplines (or, in Simon's [1957] well-known terms, they have "limited rationality"). As a result, alternative organizational forms have arisen to accommodate the needs for linking and coordinating the different parts of the typical academic organization. Further, while from some ideal perspective a completely rational governance mechanism[8] (following from contingency theory) could be imagined to replace or supplement hierarchical forms, in point of fact, political influences also cause departures from rationality in both process and structures. The configuration of the resultant governance structures redounds to the benefit of the more successful shapers of the structure (Pfeffer, 1978). It is useful to briefly outline these political considerations here, as well as in greater detail in Chapter 4.

Power in Organizations

Both the structure and culture of organizations change gradually as environments shift and different coalitions wax and wane in power. The sources of the power are themselves derived ultimately from the nature of the environment that the institution faces, and that shifting environment determines "critical contingencies" — for example, shortages of such resources as funds or information (Salancik & Pfeffer, 1977). Those units or persons that can best attend to the contingencies will be found to have power — not only to garner benefits for themselves, but, within limits, to change aspects of the structure and the norms themselves that will increase and perpetuate that power. Decision-making structures, representing dispersions of authority and power, reflect the current critical contingencies being experienced by colleges and universities and can thus be seen as

---

8. We refer here to Mannheim's conception of "functional" rationality — i.e., the condition of organizational action that is judged to serve definite organizational goals and can be "calculated" by an outside observer (Mannheim, 1940).

rational organizational adaptations modified by the product of conflicts over power—that is, by the current dominant coalition. Indeed, to the extent that power accrues to holders of positions that are truly critical to organizational functioning, the shift in structure to accommodate power holders may itself be efficient, not irrational.[9] Understanding "governance" and the dispersion of authority in colleges and universities in these terms would seem then to be a more apt and parsimonious explanation than that commonly proposed—namely, governance as a unique form of decision-making structure suited only to equally unique institutions of higher education.

A further word is necessary here concerning the meaning of the term "power" as used in this book. I intend to convey through this term both a latent informal structural property of organizations, as well as a process. By informal structure, I mean individuals or aggregates of individuals (e.g., in coalitions) that are not recognized formally by the organization in its table of organization or description of positions and responsibilities. Power as a structural property of organizations, then, reflects a static (i.e., relatively permanent as opposed to *ad hoc*) condition of asymmetrical relationships among participants in an organization. I also will refer in this book to power as a process. In this sense, I mean the activities of members of an organization as these reflect attempts to impose nonrational (or non-bureaucratic) solutions to organizational problems on other organizational members. This is not to say that such efforts are (necessarily) contrary to the willingness of the other members to accept these solutions; it is only to say that the political process is here defined in a more limited way as simply the attempt to create other than rational, bureaucratic solutions.[10]

Organizational Design

All complex organizations are formally structured to some degree. They are arrangements of individual workers into groups—the particular arrangements presumed to be those that maximize effective-

---

9. Of course, "politics" frequently involves the creation of the illusion of urgency, and adept politicians can often exert influence in excess of the organizational justification for it.

10. This more limited notion was chosen instead of the usual definition of power as the capacity to influence others against their "will." The confusion in the literature on this subject (see, e.g., Astley & Sachdeva, 1984) leads to a narrower conceptual framework.

ness and efficiency (or at least presumed not to contravene blatantly the myth of an institution-wide goal of effectiveness and efficiency). The major question is why the functional prerequisites noted above have been accommodated in the modern college or university by structures different from the more typical bureaucratic one, with its accompanying culture. Why, in other words, has the structure of academic departmentalization arisen as the primary mode of division of labor and why has the special coordinating mode — the governance structure through which authority is dispersed — been adopted? The almost universal presence of the discipline-based department has been explained elsewhere (Bess, 1971, 1973b, 1982). Here the concern is with the explanation of the second part of the question — namely, the contingencies that explain the presence of governance as a framework for decision making.

One typical answer reported in the literature is that academic enterprises constitute a unique kind of professional organization, marked especially by an extreme rationalistic bias on the part of most individuals and by a tradition of professional autonomy defended by academic freedom. Because of the heterogeneity of academic fields and their personnel, it is alleged, a "collegial" courtesy, manifested as a strong set of norms (Parsons, 1971) has evolved into an almost ubiquitous formal structure for decision making, which is called a "senate" or "academic council." Combined with a comparably genial stance on the bureaucratic side, consensus can be reached and decisions taken. The idea persists, then, that decision making in academic matters is in some way bound up in a courtly dance of deference and participation called collegiality.

In point of fact, the idea of collegiality, while long-standing, has a variety of meanings, none of which fully explains academic decision making. Indeed, different interpretations of collegiality are called upon depending on the occasion and the needs of the declarer. For some, it is a set of norms and values making up an academic culture; for others, it is a structure for decision making; and for still others, it is a pattern of interaction among faculty and administration. In Chapter 5 of this book, some of the ambiguities about collegiality are unraveled in an effort to simplify and clarify both what it is and what purposes it serves. It may be, for example, that collegiality as a normative condition in higher education probably is not widespread, except in rudimentary forms of wishes and hopes for cooperation and a structure for exchanging worries and promises. On the other hand, there are some participatory rights (or rites) that may distinguish decision making in higher education from that in other organizations, including those in the profit-making sector. Plenary meetings of the faculty senate, for example, are unusual decision-making forms and constitute an uncommon structure for decision making. There are few comparable nonpolitical (i.e., organizational) enterprises where recourse is routinely made to a large group of line workers.[11] More typically, decisions of a policy nature are made by an executive coterie or even by a single officer (e.g., the chief executive officer). Of course, there is some question as to whether "policy" is indeed shaped by such academic councils (e.g., see, Lindblom, 1959; Mintzberg, 1979; Hardy et al., 1984). Nevertheless, the faculty senate does exist. Its organizational rationale must be explained not by claims to the uniqueness of the academic profession but by the use of traditional organizational theory. The recourse to collective decision making, in other words, can be seen as a response to common organizational problems whose solutions are met in a variety of ways in different types of organizations. The recourse, then, is common, though the particular dimensions of the structural solution may not be.

Let me illustrate somewhat further. In decision-making bodies like senates (and their related committee structures), attention is paid to the four key general systems domains noted earlier in this chapter—namely, inputs (funds, raw material, personnel), transformation processes, outputs, and feedback, as these are managed in the course of satisfying the four Parsonian functional prerequisites. To understand how the authority for overseeing these functions is dispersed over the structures and role occupants requires a deeper analysis of the processes themselves, particularly from the more abstract perspective of organizations in general, rather than colleges and universities as unique entities.

The approach for the remainder of the book will be to focus on the domains of decision making—inputs, transformation processes, outputs, and feedback—and to search for explanations of the dispersion of authority over these domains. For example, for two of the more general concerns of the book—information flow and coordination—patterns of college and university decision-making structures in the four systems domains will be examined. In Chapters 2 and 3, "rational" (read "nonpolitical" or nomothetic) explanations of deci-

---

11. Possible exceptions are large-scale industrial democracies and small settings with "quality circles." Union votes under collective bargaining might also be construed as similar, but in those cases decisions are usually not concerned with strategic matters.

sion making will be sought. At the conclusion of the discussion of information flow and coordination, I will introduce the notion of power as a confounding influence and demonstrate how a rational dispersion (i.e., one justified in terms of a presumably commonly shared set of organizational objectives) is compromised through the influence of the "coalitions," which do not presuppose common objectives. In Chapter 5, the subject of collegiality as a cultural, structural, and behavioral phenomenon that influences the dispersion of authority is considered. In particular, the values of rationality and trust will be seen to affect the shape of the structures in each of the decision domains.

A model describing the various concepts of interest and their hypothesized relationships appears in Figure 1.4.

Figure 1.4
Sources of the Dispersion of Authority in Colleges and Universities

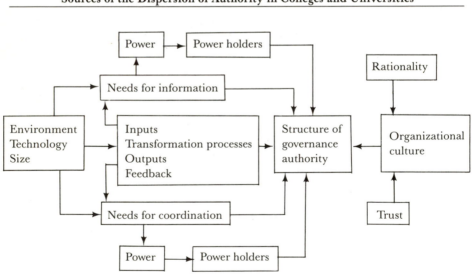

CHAPTER

TWO *Authority Structures and Vertical Information Flow*

All organizations are primarily concerned with the management of uncertainty as they attempt to achieve their goals, however these may be defined. In some organizations with known technologies and stable environments, uncertainty is controlled by the circumscription of subordinates' range of decision making. In other organizations facing more turbulent settings, the attempt is made to limit the influence of the uncertainties of the environment (e.g., through the development of multiple product lines that rely on different customers). In still other organizations, "buffering strategies" and "bridging strategies" (Scott, 1981, p. 190ff) are employed. Central to the management of uncertainty is the propitious provision of appropriate information to decision makers. Overloading or underloading decision makers or providing unusable information creates conditions for decision making that cause employee uncertainty and lead to errors of commission or omission (cf. Driver, 1984).

Information flows in many directions in organizations—across boundaries (in and out) and internally (up and down, and diagonally). Of interest here is the management of internal information flows in the organizational hierarchy of the modern college or university. In this chapter, the vertical flow of information is considered; in the next, horizontal flows. In each case, the concern is with understanding how and why the structure of decision making has evolved in response to the struggle to manage the uncertainty of information that is characteristic in these types of institutions.

One useful framework for understanding the information processing contingencies that enter into the emergence and/or design of organizational structure comes from the work of Galbraith (1977), whose approach seems to fit well the special "knowledge shaped" character of colleges and universities. (cf. Khandwalla, 1977; Nadler & Tushman, 1978). Galbraith's basic proposition is that task uncertainty dictates to a considerable extent the kind of authority structures that emerge in organizations. He notes, "the greater the task uncertainty, the greater the amount of information that must be processed among decision makers during task execution in order to achieve a given level of performance" (p. 36). As will be shown below, control of information is a basic mode of acquiring power, leading, in turn, to personal gain, which may or may not be coincident with organizational effectiveness (cf. Crozier, 1964; Hickson et al., 1971; Pfeffer, 1980). Hence, the design of organizations can be understood partly in terms that show how the dominant coalition manipulates the structure (e.g., in colleges and universities, the governance mechanisms) to control information sources and flow, thereby reducing uncertainty (or at least giving the illusion of reducing it). The definition of "information" also falls to the dominant coalition. Academic governance structures must be seen, then, as necessarily information driven. The dispersion of authority can be conceived as a resultant partly of forces defining information and assessing its value.

In this chapter, the emphasis is on structural designs that meet the organization's needs for information exchange, especially up and down the organization. Upper management needs information for strategic planning in the light of changing contingencies; the "technical core" requires information about policies that link separated units; middle management must have information for the purpose of protecting the technical core from excessive buffeting from the environment (Thompson, 1967) and for dampening swings in product or service quality and output that may not match demand.

In higher education, the problem is exacerbated by the fact that faculty occupy all three levels, with the same individuals often asked to wear different hats on different occasions, depending on the type of decision. For example, at the executive level (in this case, both administrators and omnibus faculty councils) information may be needed about social and cultural change in the society served by the institution. At the managerial level, deans may seek information for the purpose of planning curricular shifts in different schools and departments; or, at the department level, chairpersons may need to make decisions about changes in specific input or output characteristics (e.g., in students, graduates, funding for research, and uses of research), which may require other types of information. At the technical core, faculty teaching and research demand still other kinds of information.

The most common structure that organizations develop to address their information processing needs is a hierarchy of offices, each level of which carries authority over the one below. This is largely represented by Kilmann's "operational" design, outlined earlier. Other methods of dealing with internal, vertical information exchange needs are decentralization and goal setting, which will be considered later.

Hierarchies are functional in that they tend to identify more clearly where the authority lies, to reduce the number of communication channels needed, and to connect interdependent units (Galbraith, 1977, p. 43). However, hierarchies tend to have serious limitations, especially for organizations in which interdependencies exist among units and where technological uncertainties demand frequent, unstructured communication among members of different groups. In universities, for example, development of a new course by one department may require interaction with a variety of other departments, none of which has formal bureaucratic connections with the originating department. Or, an accreditation visit may require communications among departments and administrative units not usually considered interdependent.

The channels for communication in a hierarchy are few and limited in information-carrying capacity. Moreover, each position technically is connected only with those above and below. Hence, whenever problems arise that are unanticipated or for which there are no known technologies (cf. Perrow's discussions of technology, 1970, pp. 50ff), the channels become overloaded, and delays and distortions occur. As the number of exceptions to routine decision making increases, the capacity of the hierarchy to handle them is exceeded. To mitigate these circumstances, organizations develop regularized patterns of decision making. "Governance" mechanisms in higher education, for example, can be understood in part as a structural accommodation to the information overload or distortion problems that occur in any traditional hierarchy. Some of the substructures of academic governance are visible and stable mechanisms for routine decision making. They can—and should—be conceived of as hierarchical, if not bureaucratic, despite the fact that they exist in the framework of an allegedly "collegial" structure. Other substructures are designs that stray from the bureaucratic (or, again in Kilmann's terms, from the "operational") and are shaped to handle exceptional problems. As Kilmann points out (1977, pp. 36–41), the orientations of the persons operating these nonbureaucratic structures differ, or should differ, to maximize effectiveness. Some *ad hoc* committees, for example, often are not part of the formal bureaucracy. Those that are formed to deal with the more profound or organizational problems are staffed by faculty whose orientations differ from those who sit on the more routine committees. Or, if the orientations do not differ, the solutions to the problems addressed by the *ad hoc* committees will tend to be bureaucratic ones, as committee members receive and process information with a view primarily toward internal efficiency and control. Many a shrewd dean has seen fit to "stack" committees with personnel who are likely to arrive at the solution desired by the dean (though the dean is more likely to use values and attitudes more than personality as a basis for committee membership).

In some nonprofit organizations, rules and procedures for management of uncertainty can be developed by stretching the bureaucracy only slightly. In colleges and universities, on the other hand, because a majority of key product or service design decisions (e.g., curriculum changes) are made on a decentralized basis in academic departments, and because the numbers of products or services offered by the institution are diverse (i.e., there are numerous departments), many decisions that would ordinarily be referred upward in a hierarchy cannot be so accommodated. Each decision becomes virtually unique or exceptional. As Perrow (1970) noted, a hierarchical form of organization cannot deal efficiently with such a pattern of diversity. Instead, either more decentralization must take place—up to the limit where coordination of technological interdependencies is threatened—or other structures (e.g., senates) must arise to fill that need. Among those other structures in higher education is the university collegial decision-making apparatus. Why this structure is efficient for decision making in universities can be explained using some of Galbraith's theory on information exchange.

Responses to Information Overload

Galbraith indicates that organizations typically may react to information overload problems in two ways: (1) they may reduce the amount of information that is processed; and (2) they may increase the capacity of the organization to handle more information. Three methods, in turn, are proposed to accomplish the first of the above: (a) environmental management; (b) creation of slack resources; and (c) creation of self-contained tasks. Two others are used in the second mode: (a) investment in vertical information systems; and (b) creation of lateral relations. In Figure 2.1, these five methods are arrayed

Figure 2.1
Structural Approaches to Improved Information Management
for Different Types of Decisions (Galbraith Framework)

DECISION DIMENSIONS	REDUCTION IN NEED FOR INFORMATION PROCESSING			INCREASE IN CAPACITY FOR INFORMATION PROCESSING	
	Environmental Management	*Creation of Slack Resources*	*Creation of Self-contained Tasks*	*Investment in Vertical Information Systems*	*Creation of Lateral Relations*
Inputs	1	5	9	13	17
Transformations	2	6	10	14	18
Outputs	3	7	11	15	19
Feedback	4	8	12	16	20

against the four central decisions outlined in Chapter 1, yielding 20 foci for discussion.

In other words, for each of the decision dimensions (inputs, transformations, outputs, and feedback) there are five potential modes for improving information management. As will be seen, not all of these methods of information management are found in equal measure in the strategies available to colleges and universities. Let us consider each separately.

Environmental Management

The first way that any organization can act to reduce the information-processing demands on its system is to seek to manage its environment more effectively. That is, the organization can seek to reduce its uncertainty about events that are critical to its functioning. Note that this changes the "contingencies" for the organization, moving it from an unstable to a stable environment, thus making a bureaucratic form of structure more efficient. Scott (1981) refers in this connection to "buffering" activities that protect the technical core (cf. Thompson, 1967). These include such techniques as coding, stockpiling, leveling, forecasting, and growth (expanding the technical core).

Let us examine this activity in higher education, looking at its bureaucratic side only and exploring how it might be made more effective through environmental management. First, the system's "input" domain is considered. In this instance, the college or university could attempt to stabilize (or at least render variations more predictable in) any or all of the three input dimensions noted earlier: (1) funds; (2) students and knowledge brought into the system; and (3) faculty or staff entering into the organization. This would require, in the first case, that it attempt to ensure a continuity of grant and tuition income. In the second case, it would mean that efforts be organized to ensure a more predictable (though not necessarily more stable) level of student demand and that the state of the knowledge industry be controlled and ordered more efficiently for faculty use. And, in the third instance, the college or university would have to improve its recruiting techniques so that not only was the supply of human resources assured but quality remained stable and at the desired levels. Each of these measures would make it more possible for traditional hierarchical methods of organizational decision making to proceed more efficiently through a reduction in information uncertainty and through bureaucratic information processing.

Similar reasoning can be applied to the two other dimensions that deal with cross-boundary matters — outputs and feedback. For example, educational institutions could try to establish much more closely articulated relationships with institutions that utilize college graduates (e.g., industry, government). This kind of managed economy is, of course, characteristic of a number of centrally controlled nations or oligopolistic industries. With respect to feedback domains, it is conceivable that colleges and universities could set up more sensitive indicators of the degree of acceptance of their products and services, thus permitting more accurate and rapid organizational adaptation to needed change. In each of these domains, management of the environment would result in a reduction of the information-processing strains on a traditional hierarchy, rendering it more efficient.

While it could be argued that colleges and universities might do much more along these lines to strengthen the efficiency of their bureaucracies, it would appear that most of the environmental conditions are beyond the control of the organization (i.e., the input domain is presently more volatile than usual), or, of more interest in this chapter, are deemed so by the dominant coalition. That is, not only will strong interest groups in the college argue that little further can be done to ensure more stability in the environment, but they will point to other organizational mechanisms that will, allegedly more effectively, reduce the pressures on the administrative hierarchy for more information processing. Indeed, they will argue that in the absence of the ability to control the environment, other means, such as extant governance structures, must be called into play.[1] These arguments, of course, from the perspective of contingency theory may lead to increased organizational efficiency at the same time that they may serve the interests of the coalition in power.

Increasing Slack Resources

The second mode for reducing the load on hierarchical structures for information processing is, according to Galbraith (1977), the creation of "slack resources," which are the excess of inputs (defined earlier as required funds, raw material, and personnel) over what is required to perform the tasks at hand. Slack resources in a college or university might include budget surpluses, faculty in excess of the course requirements of the curriculum, and more laboratories than are needed. Traditional ways of producing organizational slack involve the more aggressive or enlightened search for sufficient input resources, which has been receiving considerable attention at virtually every educational institution in recent years.

Another approach to achieving a condition of slack resources is to reduce the organization's level of performance. Thus, for example, a college might accept fewer raw material inputs (students) to be processed or reduce the quality requirements of the transformation processes (e.g., offer fewer but larger courses). While such a condition is costly because these idle resources are not productive, it does reduce the needs for tightly controlled and timely information processing. For example, with excess faculty, it is not as necessary to be sure that enrollments do not exceed available sections of a class, since through bureaucratic procedures (either an algorithm in a policy manual or an assistant dean who is authorized to make the decision), extra sections can be added and plentiful faculty easily assigned. As Galbraith notes:

---

1. It should be noted, of course, that neither the "dominant coalition" nor the arguments from them are to be construed as invariably overt. Indeed, the coalition may not even be aware of itself, of the messages it is sending, or of the rationale for the messages.

Thus the creation of slack resources, through reduced performance levels, reduces the amount of information that must be processed during task execution and prevents the overloading of hierarchical channels. Whether the organization chooses this strategy or not depends on the relative costs of the other four strategies for handling the overload. (1977, p. 50)

As with the first strategy (environmental management), this one is also not likely to be readily adopted in higher education. Clearly, it is quite difficult in times of budgetary constraints to create slack. In colleges and universities where budget reductions have followed enrollment declines, administrators and sometimes faculty are in short supply as lost faculty personnel lines are not replaced. In the latter case, administrators are hard put to manage the curricular and faculty assignment issues that come up at the last minute. Information overload pressures on the traditional hierarchical system do, therefore, arise and must be managed, in the Galbraith model, through the creation of structures alternative to the hierarchy.

On the other hand, in situations where, despite financial stress, tenure has created conditions of excess faculty, the organization has, perhaps inadvertently, created a different kind of organizational slack. In this latter and more common situation, curricular and faculty loads may be adjusted through an existing administrative hierarchy that can more efficiently manage the flow of information. This may explain in part why faculty in recent times report that power appears to be shifting upward and outward. The administrative hierarchy, in the presence of organizational slack, is increasingly able to make decisions brought on by information uncertainties.

Creation of Self-Contained Tasks

The third mode of reducing the information-processing strain on the bureaucratic hierarchy in organizations is, according to Galbraith, the creation of self-contained tasks. By reducing the number of independent specialists contributing to a task, the need for exchange among specialists is reduced. This can be accomplished either by physically aggregating specialists together for ease of communication (eliminating the need for both lateral communication across departments and vertical supervisory control) or by creating more generalists — personnel who can perform more than a single specialty (cf. Tyler, 1973). Thus, the communication across specialized tasks is performed internally by the person him- or herself. The effect of these adjustments is to have "the point of decision moved closer to the source of information. Exceptions have to travel through fewer levels before reaching a shared superior. Decisions can be made at lower levels, supported by only local information" (Galbraith, 1973, p. 27).

It is in this domain that the information-processing perspective proposed by Galbraith is perhaps most helpful in explaining the presence of extra- or supra-hierarchical decision-making frameworks (such as senates and faculty committees) in colleges. The organizational model of self-contained academic departments that exists in most colleges and universities is not only a rational response to the division of research labor brought on by disciplinary specialization (cf. Bess, 1982), but is also the latent response of the faculty as a whole (and of the dominant coalition) to the alleged inability of the hierarchical system to handle all of the information required for efficient decision making. For example, it is claimed that deans and vice presidents are incapable of comprehending the differences in disciplines and thus can neither intervene in departmental production (transformation) matters nor evaluate faculty performance.

Thus, the creation of self-contained tasks—the circumscription of domains of research in particular around the departmental structure and the circumscription of domains of productivity in general (i.e., the three major roles of teaching, research, and service) around the individual faculty member—serves to reduce the information-processing responsibilities of the hierarchical system in colleges and universities. The allocation of decision-making authority to the department and to the faculty in general follows, then, not simply from the traditions of academic freedom and professional peer control but from the organizational requirement that a hierarchical system not be overburdened with decisions that it is not equipped to handle.

Just as with the first two modes of structural accommodation to information-processing needs—environmental management and creation of slack resources—so also with creation of self-contained tasks, we can understand the evolution of commonly found university decision-making structures as a rational organizational response to the problem of dealing with perceived uncertainty. The diagnosis is facilitated by looking once again at the four decision domains—inputs, transformation processes, outputs, and feedback. For example, control over student inputs (admissions) at the undergraduate level is, in most colleges, a centralized operation. The reason is that through bureaucratic rules (e.g., admissions standards and policies that reduce the number of exceptions that have to be processed), the administrative hierarchy can manage the information flow problems without incurring an overload.

On the other hand, in graduate education, where it is important that there be much communication about who should or should not be admitted—presumably because more homogeneity is needed in raw material (students)—the process is managed through the self-contained departments themselves. Similarly, when input decisions concerning new faculty (recruitment or tenure decisions) are required, the nature of the information is again often exceptional—that is, it does not permit routine bureaucratic processing without an enormous elaboration of rules and regulations to cover multiple contingencies. Hence, the mode adopted in most colleges and universities is to create self-contained units (departments) in which are aggregated all of the human sources of information (the faculty) that can make the decision much more efficiently.[2] Transformation processes (research and teaching) as well as outputs and feedback can be shown also to require a dispersion of authority to structures other than the hierarchy, again because of the need to reduce information-processing stresses.

Investment in Vertical Information Systems

As noted earlier, Galbraith proposed five alternative organizing modes for improving the capacity of an organizational hierarchy to handle exceptional decisions. The three discussed above were concerned with reducing the need for information processing. The final two modes call for increasing the capacity of the system to manage information. They are "investment in vertical information systems" and "creation of lateral relations."

An investment in the vertical information system will result in an improvement in the flow of information up and down the hierarchy. The organization can thus make better use of the information acquired in the course of executing its tasks and can, in turn, consider in an informed way improvements both in transformation processes and in organizational design. Several mechanisms can be employed to accomplish this purpose, according to Galbraith. These have to do with the decision frequency, scope of the data base, degree of formal-

---

2. The reasons for administrative oversight of these decisions are discussed later.

ization of the information flows, and capacity of the decision mechanism to process information.[3]

The first organizational option for improving information flow through investment in the vertical system has to do with changes in the length of time between decisions. As the frequency of decisions required in the administrative hierarchy increases, some means must be employed to prevent the system from falling behind and/or making errors. One such means, according to Galbraith, is the scheduling of more frequent planning meetings. The more frequent the meetings, the more quickly bureaucratic policies can be changed, and the fewer exceptions will be referred upward. While more meetings are costly in terms of personnel time, they are less so than the alternatives of slack resources or self-contained structures.

Applied to colleges and universities, the model demonstrates why there is apparent pressure for ever-increasing numbers of meetings (or so faculty claim). The reason is that the administration needs information in order to change its bureaucratic rules to adapt to rapidly shifting conditions. Unfortunately, the unique faculty role structure in academia makes it difficult to use increased numbers of meetings to make the shifts efficiently. As Etzioni (1961) points out, faculty are at once both line and staff personnel. In their teaching and research capacities, faculty act as line personnel, while in their recruiting and promoting roles, they play the parts usually reserved for staff personnel in the profit-making sector. In industry, for example, meetings are a common mode of decision making for staff, but line personnel are tethered to the ineluctable flow of inputs to be transformed on schedule. So also in higher education, faculty qua line personnel cannot be spared from their direct transformation tasks (e.g., teaching, research) without serious impairment of the flow of finished products or services. Hence, faculty (or at least most faculty) will resist increases in committee assignments and meetings. They are also dispositionally not inclined toward this type of involvement in organizational decision making, academic work typically requiring primarily individual, not group, decision making. In any case, the mode of increasing the frequency of meetings is not an adjustment commonly found in colleges and universities.

The second dimension in the option to invest in vertical information systems is the scope of the data base available to the decision system. In order to assure a smooth and tight coupling between

---

3. Because of space limitations, all four decision domains will not be considered for each of these structural or processual changes.

units, the data base can be either specialized in language or global (i.e., employing the language and data of all the subunits at once). Which one depends on the interdependencies among the subunits. If subunits require close tolerances, as in functionally structured organizations or in systems in which sequential rather than pooled interdependence obtains, then managements must invest in information systems that are global. Since for a variety of reasons discipline-oriented academic departments are autonomous, interdependence is pooled and the data bases of the hierarchical systems connecting them tend to be more local. Although such pooled interdependence is artificial and inefficient for the teaching mission (Bess, 1982), it persists, making recourse to a global data base unavailable. As a result, institutions of higher learning have had to erect a decision-making apparatus that uses live personnel, rather than dead, computerized data.

More clearly, the committee structure and other senate governance mechanisms are the organizational response to the need for investment in vertical information systems that employ global data base systems. But instead of stored common data, the information system comprises faculty members who provide the data needed for decisions on an *ad hoc* basis, thus accounting for the apparently idiosyncratic and exceptional nature of the decisions to be made. The organization thus also experiences pressure for more frequent meetings in this second option to invest in a vertical information system. In this case, however, the faculty are more likely to comply, since a global data base requires their input and they can control for their own purposes the data about their operations that is entered into the data base. A faculty member in the department of psychology, for example, would rather participate in a committee meeting on the need for statistical literacy among undergraduates than submit complete curricular and course information about the teaching of statistics in her department.

The third dimension of the design option of investing in vertical information systems is "formalization." As the hierarchical system becomes overloaded, it will break down unless some means of standardizing the seemingly disparate bits of information is developed. As Galbraith notes:

> The primary effect of the formalized languages is to permit the transmission of information with fewer symbols thereby expanding the communications channels to carry more information. The ability of an organization to coordinate diverse outputs across specialized resources

depends critically upon having an efficient means to identify all the factors and record changes to them in the face of uncertainty. (1977, p. 99)

Translated to the academic arena, the need is for some standardized terminology that can convey meaningfully the transformation processes (teaching and research) carried out in different disciplines. Hierarchical coordination of departmental activities would be facilitated by such standardization. For example, administrators who could calculate precisely what a "unit of learning" was in each discipline would be better able to regulate the assignment of credit.

But it is manifest that in academic systems, the languages in each discipline are recondite, rendering their formalization in a standardized format virtually impossible. Hence, formalization as an avenue for improving the information-processing capacity of the formal hierarchy usually cannot be advanced (except perhaps in some input and output domains of admissions and graduation requirements, where numerical criteria common to all subunits can be utilized).

The reasons why formalization does not take place vary, depending on whether teaching or research is at issue. In the area of research, there is usually little pressure on the hierarchical system to resolve cross-disciplinary problems, since, for the most part, research is unidisciplinary. In those exceptional cases where problems arise, Galbraith (1977, p. 100) predicts that "nonformal, usually verbal, channels" will be used, and, indeed, this mode of resolution is commonly found. In the area of teaching, on the other hand, questions of curricular prerogatives do tend to require the use of hierarchical channels. Despite the presence of specialized languages as in the research area, faculty tend not to resort to informal verbal channels to deal with their curricular problems. Rather, structural solutions (e.g., senate curricular committees) are formally constituted to resolve conflicts. The illustration cited above concerning the psychology department is a case in point. The explanation lies in the domino effects of informal bilateral agreements. Curricular decisions tend to have ramifications beyond the two departments seeking to resolve a conflict. If two departments were to decide to increase the credits awarded for a standard 30-contact-hour semester course, it is certain that cries would be heard from every other department across the campus.

In sum, formalization or standardization of data in higher education does not seem to be an option for investing in the hierarchical system. Further, informal communication is eschewed (at least with regard to teaching matters), contrary to the Galbraith prediction, with academics preferring to resolve controversies through formal structures within the typical academic decision-making apparatus.

Galbraith's fourth design technique for improving information processing through investment in the vertical information system is an increase in the capacity of the decision mechanism. As this discussion overlaps somewhat with later discussions, we will delay it, except to note that the computer revolution has had profound impacts on vertical decision-making capacity, with enormous political consequences for the dominant coalition (Pfeffer, 1977).

Creation of Lateral Relations

Thus far discussed have been four of the five alternative design options in Galbraith's model for improving the flow of information and thereby reducing the strain on the hierarchy. To reiterate, the five were:

> Changing the environment
> Creating slack resources
> Increasing the degree of self-containment
> Investment in the vertical information system
> Creation of lateral relations

The first three are intended to reduce the needs of the organization for information exchange. The fourth (comprising the four elements discussed just above) and the fifth (to be discussed next) are aimed not only at reducing information needs but also at facilitating the flow of information throughout the organization.

As noted earlier, Galbraith's fifth alternative for improving the capacity of the system to process information has to do with the establishment of coordinating mechanisms across departments. Galbraith reports:

> The final organizing mode . . . is to employ lateral forms of communication and joint decision-making processes. That is, instead of referring a problem upward in the hierarchy, the managers solve the problem at their own level, contacting and cooperating with peers in those departments affected by the new information.
>
> As with the other organizing modes, the purpose is to reduce the number of decisions being referred upward. As in the case of vertical

information systems, the effect is to increase the capacity of the organization to process information and to make decisions. (1977, p. 111)

This mode is at the heart of the explanation in this book of governance in higher education. Note that the creation of lateral relations parallels in many ways but is different from the establishment of self-contained groups. Here the concern is with linkages required across specializations, where the latter can*not* be made self-contained. Discipline-oriented departmentalization in higher education is a case in point (though some would argue that other forms of organization might improve efficiency). Departments strain toward self-sufficiency (and self-control), but manage it essentially only in the research area, where they dictate inputs (knowledge), transformation processes (research methods), and outputs (publications). In other domains, they are at least partially interdependent with other units in the institution. Undergraduate and graduate inputs (admissions criteria) and outputs (graduation criteria) are determined in conjunction with other departments. Transformation decisions (e.g., curriculum and teaching) are mostly self-determined for courses offered in the major field, but shared for service courses. Whether these necessary lateral relations are handled through hierarchical means or through other structures can be understood by examining the alternatives proposed in the model.

Galbraith notes that there are a number of means of improving lateral relations, ranging from quite simple and informal direct contact across departments to the establishment of a formal "linking-managerial" role and ultimately to "matrix design." What follows is a discussion of these various methods for improving lateral relations. In the final section of this chapter is a consideration of how the four decision domains noted at the outset—inputs, transformation processes, outputs, and feedback—are addressed through the mechanisms of lateral relations.

Interestingly, informal contact across departments, at once the simplest and the most efficient means of relieving the burden on the hierarchy, is inhibited in colleges and universities by the profound differences in orientation across departments. This matter was noted above in the discussion of formalization as a mode of relieving pressures on the administrative hierarchy. Whereas in industrial concerns informal communication often takes place as a matter of course, in academic discipline-oriented departments many organizational issues that cross departmental boundaries (e.g., curriculum overlaps) are not handled informally through faculty-to-faculty contact. In part this is because of the career-long association of most faculty with one discipline and, these days, one department. This is in contrast, again, with industrial practice, especially in organizations modeled after the Japanese personnel practice of rotating most employees throughout the organization. In the latter case, long-standing friendships, or at least associations, are established, making liaisons through direct contact much easier.

The second mechanism for creating lateral relations in Galbraith's scheme is the establishment of a formal role (other than the immediate supervisor or his/her staff surrogate in the hierarchy) to adjudicate differences among departments. Such roles are not common in higher education, however, probably because of the fear of confusing an already ambiguous decision-making structure. If two sources of power—faculty and administrators—have difficulty determining how decisions should be made, it is probably true that the creation of yet another class of decision maker would further complicate an already amorphous and ambiguous decision-making process and structure.

Yet one more example of structures serving lateral process needs in organizations, says Galbraith, is the creation of "task forces [that are] a form of horizontal contact which is designed to solve problems of multiple departments" (Galbraith, 1977, p. 116). In contrast to the "standing committee" so well known in higher education circles, the task force is a temporary group that ceases to exist when the problem for which it was formed is thought to have been solved. Some university *ad hoc* committees might be considered task forces in Galbraith's scheme, if they are not routinely called for in administrative policy handbooks. For example, an *ad hoc* committee on promotion and tenure set up to deal with such matters when and if they arise is not a task force. On the other hand, the assembly of persons for the purpose of designing a new program, studying a marketing problem, or preparing for an accreditation visit are task forces of the kind Galbraith had in mind. The advantages of task forces are that they permit decisions to be made closer to the source of expertise—at lower levels in the organization—thereby taking the pressure off the vertical information-carrying medium of the formal hierarchy. A latent benefit is that if members of the task force are respected representatives of their constituencies, participatory prerogatives are less likely to be viewed as threatened.

When members of task forces find themselves engaged so heavily in their coordination roles in contrast to their regular tasks, another level of lateral structuring is called for. Identified by Galbraith as a "team," this entity comprises members who are given formal release time to meet on a routine basis. Such teams can be found at all levels of the formal hierarchy. Depending on the design of the organization (e.g., by function, product, client, geography, etc.), the teams perform their coordinating roles in different ways. A team comprising persons from different functional groups (e.g., admissions and teaching departments) would be likely to address issues of coordination across those functions, while in organizations structured by product (e.g., in a college of liberal arts) teams are needed to ensure that product overlaps or other inefficiencies are avoided.

In colleges and universities, the typical organizational design is by product or service, rather than function (Bess, 1982). Stemming from long-standing research traditions, academic departments are self-contained product/service units. They are related to one or several professional associations beyond their boundaries and have as their missions the propagation of research in the disciplines and the transmission of research-founded knowledge to graduate and undergraduate students. As noted earlier, research aims rarely need formal organizational linkages to facilitate their achievement (interdisciplinary research still representing a small minority of research activity—though see Clark, 1983). Teaching goals, on the other hand, more frequently need to be considered in their larger, macro-organizational context. While the most common practice is to suboptimize teaching goals, there are occasions when such orientations clash across departments. It is rare in higher education, however, to find an entity like a "team" in Galbraith's terms attending to such matters. The roots of a faculty member lie in his/her department, and it is only with great reluctance that one will leave academic pursuits for temporary (very short-term) full-time duty as an academic coordinator. The more common form of adjudication is thus the ubiquitous curriculum committee. In sum, creation of lateral relations, Galbraith's second form of facilitating information flow by reducing pressure on the vertical decision-making system, founders on the shoals of strong faculty allegiances to individual departments. The latter forces the organization to develop other structural mechanisms that can simultaneously recognize faculty predilections for "staying home" while at the same time meeting the need to relieve the administrative hierarchy. That this is an unhappy and inefficient accommodation is well recognized both by administrations that are often not relieved at all and by faculty for whom this kind of activity is distracting.

The central point of this extended discussion of Galbraith's model has been to point out how the organization's need for information processing in each of the four decision domains—inputs, transformation processes, outputs, and feedback—cannot be handled adequately through a formal hierarchy similar to that found in industry. However, the means that most institutions of higher education take to remedy this deficiency are quite similar to many of those found in industry—namely, the reduction of information-processing strains on the hierarchy through limitations on the amount of information that must be transmitted and an increase in the capacity of the organization to carry additional needed information. The above discussions have illustrated how each of these may work—or fail to—for each decision domain.

The design of these extra-hierarchical mechanisms, however, will not necessarily be perfectly rational. Just as in business, so also in higher education, organizational design is a product of rationality as well as of power and influence, the final configuration of the structure and value system redounding to the benefit of the strongest constituencies. Thus, the accommodation to the strain on the hierarchy through any of the five modes that Galbraith suggests can best be understood both as contingent on the environment and the technology of the transformation processes and as a response to the pressures of the dominant coalition toward self-serving, suboptimized ends or toward larger organizational objectives.

One further elaboration of this point is necessary. To the extent that faculty, or at least some faculty, represent the dominant coalition, their interpretation of "uncertainty" will drive the mechanisms that are created to reduce it. Daft and Macintosh (1981) have adapted Perrow's conceptualization of technology to take into account the needs of the system to manage uncertainty. Focusing on task uncertainty and its management, they found that uncertainty about the occurrence of problems was positively associated with the amount of information processing. Using the terminology adopted above, it might be said that the more uncertainty about the variance in inputs (i.e., either about the nature of diverse student bodies or about data required for research), the more a faculty member will engage in information-processing activity to resolve that uncertainty.

On the other hand, Daft and Macintosh discovered that when uncertainty about how to *analyze* the variance in inputs was high, there was less information processing. Again, in the terms used here, if faculty are faced with uncertainty about what procedures to use, either to teach or do research, they will, according to this hypothesis, seek resolutions of the problem in other than information-seeking ways. For example, faculty will utilize a more readily accessible repertory of behaviors, such as using old syllabuses or standard research techniques. The reason, according to Daft and Macintosh, is that "coding schemes are difficult to develop and information is difficult to share when activities are intangible and poorly understood."

Faculty reluctance to discuss the tasks of teaching can perhaps be understood, then, in terms of the difficulty of communicating poorly understood transformation processes. More important for the discussion here, however, is the notion that abstaining from lateral communication about a central organizational task forces the organization to reinterpret the task so that it appears routine or to create other structural mechanisms to deal with the uncertainty through a unit of analysis larger than the individual faculty member. In higher education, the solution is to deal with teaching in the former way and with research in the latter. We bureaucratize the teaching process by assigning specialists (admissions personnel) to deal with the variance in inputs. We rationalize the research process by retaining the departmental structure that supports it. Structures arise, then, that are simultaneously responsive to hierarchical overload and the priorities of powerful persons.

In the next chapter, yet another aspect of organizations — differentiation and integration — will be considered to determine the extent to which the variables highlighted in the literature on organizations can illuminate the structure of the decision-making processes in colleges and universities. The set of coordinating configurations resulting from the adjustments in the hierarchy will be discussed. As in the present chapter, the argument will demonstrate that the modes of integration and differentiation respond at once to organizational needs and to power. The dispersion of authority, then, through formal structure and informal system will be comprehensible in terms of both.

CHAPTER THREE

Authority Structures and Inter-Unit Coordination

In Chapter 2, the suggestion was made that vertical flows of information necessitated the creation of special bureaucratic and nonbureaucratic forms of decision making, and that college and university governance structures can be understood as organizational responses to information needs up and down the administrative hierarchy. This chapter is a continuation of the search for explanations of governance structures—this time looking at the *horizontal* flows of information required by the nature of academic work and workers. The chapter builds on the near classic theories of Lawrence and Lorsch, James Thompson, and March and Simon, then moves to the more contemporary approaches of Mintzberg and Van de Ven, Delbecq, and Koenig.

Just as with vertical information flow, where the interstices between the levels in the hierarchy are sources of distortion and load problems, so also with lateral flows, the separation of individuals and units constitutes a significant potential bottleneck. As Lawrence and Lorsch (1967) so well noted, division of labor leads inevitably to the twin structural-functional problems of differentiation and integration. When labor is divided into functional specializations designed to address different organizational needs, structural mechanisms arise to permit the newly separated entities to coordinate their activities. Many bases for separation of specializations are possible, depending, in part, on the nature of the markets, the required transformation of raw material into final product, and the necessary qualifications of the persons who work on the product. A natural gas refinery in a stable environment with well-known technologies will be quite different from a university in a turbulent environment with

considerable ambiguity about how to transform its raw material —
students or knowledge. Whatever the reasons for separation, however, once divided, the units must be united through a variety of
integrating mechanisms.

Some would suggest that the inter-unit linkages that emerge in
institutions of higher education are *sui generis*, not understandable in
general terms. Clark (1979), for example, suggests that coordination
in higher education "emerges" through informal activities, rather
than through planning.

> Faculties, departments, chairs and other operating segments of academ-
> ic systems are organized around a large number of disparate specialties.
> The parts are weakly interdependent, since the task structure generates
> systems in which operations are loosely coupled. "Coordination" then
> becomes an unusual problem. Order may be more emergent than
> planned, and stabilized by emotional and symbolic bonds as much as by
> administrative structure. (p. 251)

This *natural systems* model is derived, in part, from Gouldner (1957)
and earlier, from Barnard (1938).

It is the contention here, however, that the appearance of *ad hoc*
coordination through informal means is misleading. In point of fact,
coordination in higher education can better be understood largely as
the exercise of *formal* authority, modified, perhaps, by informal authority. The holders of formal authority for coordination can be
identified using concepts and theories readily available in the organizational behavior literature. For example, as Kochen and Deutsch
note:

> Coordination may be defined as maintenance of a class of patterns,
> specified by temporal (e.g., before–after) or spatial (e.g., to the right of)
> relations among the operations of agents or facilities.
>
> As a process, coordination is a means of directing the operation of
> units so that their joint behavior attains a specified goal with higher
> probability and at lower costs. (1980, p. 126)

Thus, coordination means patterning relationships and doing it efficiently. It is also, quite clearly, a control mechanism that ensures that
outputs of units that are interdependent attain quality levels satisfac-

tory to unit members as well as to others in the organization.[1] Both "patterning" and "control" are present in colleges and universities, and they are manifested in the organizational structures considered throughout this book.

To understand how and why the coordinating structures in colleges and universities have arisen, it is necessary to consider the antecedent conditions or determinants of the division of academic labor. Four variables enter into these equations: the origins and recent history of the academic profession; the nature and strength of the linkages of each of the divided units with the "market" forces in the environment; the character of the units involved in the coordination; and the nature of the coordinating units.

Origins of Differentiation in the Academic Profession

In universities (and most colleges), the transformation processes of teaching, research, and service have come over the last century to be accomplished by "multiple function faculty" (Charns, Lawrence, & Weisbord, 1977) in discipline-centered departments. Simply stated, faculty began as teacher-administrators and gradually acquired the research function (Bess, 1982, pp. 63ff). There was virtually no change during this period in the decision-making structure of the university, except for the increase in numbers of departments. The reason for the combination of functions in each faculty member and hence in aggregates of faculty members (in contrast, say, with a more functionally differentiated system) is that this organizational design has served best the interests of researchers, whose status and power tend to dominate the organization of research universities and, through a "trickle down effect," virtually the entire academic profession. The design of an organization for research purposes in-

---

1. However, such organizational conditions as the degree of interdependence are by no means indisputable. The extent and nature of interdependencies that are alleged actually to exist are inevitably also somewhat subject to the power of the dominant coalition. For example, the interdependence between faculty in the department of mathematics and statistics and the department of psychology is determined, in part, by the power of the members of each department to define the requisite curriculum for students in each. If the former department is powerful, psychology students probably will have to take their statistics courses in the department of mathematics and statistics, rather than in their own department. Coordinating this connection will, in turn, require some formal or informal structural arrangements.

volves what Thompson (1967, p. 54) calls "pooled interdependence"—that is, the independent contribution of separated units to the whole final unit output. Each department, in other words, produces warrantably valid research through publications, which, in total, are intended to add to the reputation of the institution as a whole. To carry out most research, members of the majority of departments have relatively little need to communicate with one another, and even less to be in touch with faculty in other departments.

The consequence of the dominance of one mission over the others in terms of organizational structure is that coordinating modes tend to support the primary mission, resulting in a slighting of the others. For example, undergraduate teaching suffers because the modes of research coordination are ill-suited to this mission. To illustrate, the instructional function must be carried out through units that are in "sequential" and/or "reciprocal" interdependence (Thompson, 1967) with one another, as students are passed among various departments required for liberal education (Bess, 1982).[2] For the institution to be effective, the linkages among departments should be carried out by staff or faculty of the organization, not by its clients—the students themselves. The latter are by definition less knowledgeable and less skilled at such integration than are faculty, who, presumably, can cross disciplinary boundaries. However, since the research mission dominates, and since coordination for research purposes requires little linkage, the coordination for teaching purposes also tends to be defended as requiring few linkages. Patterns of interaction (or non-interaction) tend to be quite stable and will be set in accordance with the hierarchy of importance of tasks to be performed. Where the dominant coalition comprises researchers, the definition of critical contingencies tends to follow their predilections. A kind of "technological politics" thus prevails. Patrick Hill (now executive vice president at Evergreen State College) acted on this premise when at the State University of New York at Stony Brook he led the establishment of "federated learning communities." He found that faculty research orientations could be utilized in the design of a successful teaching experiment that required cross-disciplinary faculty interaction.

---

2. This interdependence rests, of course, on the traditional separation of disciplines into departments. Alternative proposed structures—as at places like the University of California at Santa Cruz—would suggest other kinds of interdependence (cf. Lorsch & Allen, 1973, pp. 194ff).

"Market" as an Influence in Organizational Design

In addition to these historical forces, the "market" plays a part in determining the division of labor. To the extent that faculty in relatively autonomous departments are connected to professional organizations and other agencies across the boundaries of the university, the department's activities will be governed more by "market" conditions than by internal dynamics (Williamson, 1973; Ouchi, 1981; Clark, 1983, pp. 136ff). When properly seized upon, the opportunity to respond to potential rewards in the environment renders the institution more effective.[3] Indeed, as Kerr (1963) so insightfully observed, the "federal grant" university transformed the decision-making processes in universities by allowing faculty direct access to grants. The unit of differentiation for research purposes then (at least in the federal grant universities) shifted from the department to the individual faculty member. With it came autonomy and a reinforcement of the tradition of academic freedom in the classroom. In other words, the market influence in research funding changed the basis of the division of labor, not only for research but also to some extent for teaching.

More recently, however, with demographic pressures creating serious shortages in numbers of students in some fields, and with funding sources drying up, the market has played another role. The pendulum has reversed direction. The unit of division of labor has moved upward from the faculty member to the department and even to the division or school. Despite the self-serving, if understandable, proclivities of departments to earn credits for their own departments by forcing students to take more courses in their majors, in many institutions consolidations and reconstitutions of departments have taken place as the institutions scramble to find ways both to utilize faculty and to accommodate students efficiently. In short, the division of labor in response to market forces now takes somewhat different forms.

Changes in market conditions, especially in organizations particularly sensitive to them, thus cause a concomitant recasting of the forms of departmentalization. Under conditions of market domination, the coordination moves in either of two directions. When times are good, and organizational slack exists, less coordination is needed. When the external resources are lacking, the institution is in-

---

3. For the moment, we take a unidimensional view of organizational effectiveness, recognizing that there are other ways of conceiving of it.

duced (perhaps seduced) to move toward bureaucratic means of ensuring that a continuity of services is delivered to its various markets. This happens even if tighter controls actually *reduce* rapid adaptation by decentralized units that could be autonomously responsive. When multiple subunits are mutually involved through related tasks, however, a coordinated form of adaptation is called for.

To be maximally efficient, universities must find ways of linking units whose fortunes are joined in cooperative ventures—most obviously, in producing a graduating student whose knowledge and skills have been built through the combined efforts of many departments. In point of fact, however, some universities obviate this necessity by creating the illusion of "value added." They ensure output quality by controlling input (admissions). Indeed, institutions reputed to be of *lesser* quality will be found to spend more time on coordination issues because they are less able to substitute input quality for output quality.

Faced with the need for bureaucratic control, universities historically have created a variety of mechanisms to link departments—however minimal the perceived or actual need for that linkage. To reiterate the central thesis of this book, these and other governance operations in higher education can be explained as an adaptation of a general organizational model to special problems in academia (i.e., as the most efficient decision-making mode suitable for academic professionals and different from other organization models only in the strength of the dimensions not in the dimensions themselves). The discussion that follows is intended to demonstrate the parsimony of this approach.

Contingency Approaches to Organizational Design

As noted in Chapter 1, in discussing why certain forms of coordination have arisen, therefore, it is necessary to understand them as partially rational allocations of authority and partially power-driven dispersions of influence. Using the systems approach outlined earlier, one can view coordination as a manifestation of the dispersion of power and authority over four domains: (1) inputs (funds, raw material, and personnel); (2) technological processes (teaching, research, and service); (3) outputs (graduates, publications); and (4) feedback. Needs for coordination vary across these domains. The particular type of coordination that ultimately evolves is contingent primarily on the nature of the interdependence of the subunits (Thompson,

1967, pp. 55–56), which are themselves contingent on other conditions—most particularly, the nature of the environment and the degree to which the technology employed is well established. Attempts by university organizations to impose bureaucratic coordination modes are considered next.

Hierarchical modes of coordination are found more commonly in nonacademic settings, where bureaucracies fit the more stable/simple nature of the environments and the less professionalized working staffs. Under these conditions, through planning, flows of raw materials can be anticipated with some certainty, and interdepartmental connections can be specified well in advance. On the other hand, under conditions where single departments serve multiple environments, each with varied states of turbulence, modes of coordination other than hierarchies are likely to arise. A similar line of reasoning applies to technological imperatives. Bureaucratic coordination is more likely to be found in organizations where the technology is well known and transformation processes can proceed smoothly and without exceptions requiring unusual decisions. The bureaucratic approach to coordination—"programming"—has been characterized by March and Simon (1958) as one of two possible modes (the other being "feedback"). Programming consists of anticipating the interdependencies and the critical dimensions of the connections among departments and then setting up impersonal, standardized rules of procedure. Once established, these procedures become codified and constitute guidelines for action for each unit in the interdependent relationship.

For purposes of illustration, it is helpful to explore the feasibility of this option for one of the domains of activity noted above—transformation processes. Assume for the moment a relatively stable environment and a single known technology for universities. Under these conditions, if the nature of the interdependencies that are found among departments is examined, it is possible to determine the feasibility of a decision by "programming." In particular, the "curriculum" or curricular decision making can be viewed in detail at both the departmental and institution level. (Note that curricular decisions are decisions about "technology"; that is, they deal with modes of transforming the raw material [students] who are processed through the system.)

The decision to coordinate by the programming option might in this case involve the development of procedures manuals that specify the form of syllabus to be prepared, the precise manner for delineating and measuring the achievement of course objectives, the criteria for prerequisites, and so forth. Obviously, some schools and colleges, particularly at the community college level, have already moved in this direction.

Under programmed coordination, the discretion accorded to the faculty member in the design of the course or to the department in the design of the curriculum is circumscribed by central office directives. The imposition of standardization, rules, formalization, and routinization — the usual accoutrements of bureaucratization — is done partly to control employee behavior (and hence quality of output) and partly to permit authorities to monitor the needs for change. As Perrow (1972) notes, if the nature of the raw material inputs to the organization can be made uniform (or can be assumed to be uniform) and the search procedures for analyzing the transformation requirements can be easily accessed, then the organization shifts from a craft or engineering or nonroutine type of organization to a more routine, bureaucratic one. As stronger external demands for efficiency are encountered, an increased strain toward programmed coordination can be found. The point here is that the *assumptions* about the technology of the tasks — teaching and research — commonly argue for a mode of coordination in higher education that is not programmable.[4]

There are long-standing and strong sources of resistance to such programming modes of coordination in higher education. One is the reluctance of faculty to relinquish their professional prerogatives (rephrased, to disperse their authority) to design their courses uniquely. The other is the latent realization that the specification of tasks almost automatically shifts power out of the faculty realm and into the bureaucratic or administrative. In addition, rule-based organizations tend to incur costs of surveillance (Gouldner, 1954; Pfeffer, 1978, p. 51). Hence, relatively less coordination at the more complex, institutionally differentiated institutions (i.e., universities as contrasted with community colleges) may be found. Instead, rituals and myths about education often develop to justify faculty demands for other kinds of coordination (Pfeffer, 1978, p. 103; cf. Meyer & Rowan, 1977).

In another approach to understanding the kinds and sources of coordination in organizations, Mintzberg (1983b, pp. 4ff) notes that

---

4. Whether, indeed, much teaching can be done through more mechanistic means and can thus be coordinated more bureaucratically remains both an empirical and a political question. Again, it is "assumed" that organic forms of organizational design are more appropriate for academic institutions.

there are five major linking options. Arranged in terms of the systems framework outlined in earlier chapters, they are listed below (with the system element noted in parentheses following the description):

1. Mutual adjustment — informal communication among workers. Here the organization relies on the interest and willingness of employees to seek each other out as the work requires it. (Transformational processes)
2. Direct supervision — direct oversight by one person over one or more others. In this case, the organization controls the behavior of workers directly by monitoring activities to ensure conformity to organizational objectives. (Transformational processes)
3. Standardization of work procedures — specification of the procedures involved in the transformation processes. This mode of coordination ensures desired work quality by carefully delimiting the range of acceptable employee behavior. (Transformational processes)
4. Standardization of outputs — specification of the criteria of acceptable products or services. Quality control is ensured through this method by holding employees accountable for the final product. (Outputs)
5. Standardization of worker skills, attitudes, and knowledge. By hiring workers with known characteristics, the organization need not specify either procedures or outputs, nor need it supervise, since workers can be relied on to exercise their acknowledged skills. (Inputs)

Mintzberg's observations concern the manner of control of workers within a given unit, rather than between units, which is the concern of this chapter. Nevertheless, it is necessary to observe the characteristic patterns of intra-departmental control in order fully to understand the cross-departmental coordination mechanisms. For example, as will be seen, the coordination mode most commonly found in higher education is number 5 — standardization of faculty characteristics.

Methods 2, 3, and 4 are most characteristic of bureaucratic or programming modes of coordination. However, it is quite evident that with respect to transformation functions or processes (teaching, research, and service), higher education abjures methods 2 and 3.

Faculty as prototypical professionals are not supervised directly, nor are their work processes specified. (In Chapter 5, indirect supervision through the "structure" of collegiality is discussed.) So also is method 4 problematic. Since output goals for both teaching and research in education are ambiguous and difficult to operationalize, it would appear that control over unit output is unworkable (notwithstanding informal assumptions among faculty with respect to grading standards).

The coordination modes most frequently found in higher education are 5 and 1 — standardization of faculty characteristics and mutual adjustment. The latter, however, is employed most often only in nonroutine or emergency situations, since faculty needs for communication about teaching and research are "alleged" to be infrequent. With respect to mode 5, faculty are socialized and trained as professionals in graduate schools (Bess, 1978), thereby ensuring a relatively high level of homogeneity of skills in academic institutions of similar quality. In addition, faculty are screened prior to employment at any one institution, a practice that standardizes input skills still further according to particular institutional and departmental criteria. These procedures permit the organization some confidence in presuming that its standards are being applied universally. (Also, as noted earlier, input standardization of student raw material helps control outputs on the teaching side.[5]) In sum, of these five modes of coordination, higher education seems to rely most prominently on controlling the entering skills and attitudes of its teaching-research staff. While mutual adjustment is manifested through the promulgation of the importance of collegiality, in practice, it is little used as a coordinating mode.

In point of fact, however, Mintzberg's list of coordination mechanisms slights somewhat the role of professional incentive as an ingredient of coordination. Of the first five modes, 3, 4, and 5 rely on organizational actions prior to the transformation processes. Modes 1 and 2 demand real-time monitoring of the processes, with adjustments made either at the worker's behest or by decision of the supervisor. In higher education, on the other hand, control over worker behavior comes also through the carrot of professional incentives, both extrinsic and intrinsic. Faculty desires to emulate role model peers create the "pull," rather than the "push" to conform, a phenomenon common in professional as contrasted with bureaucratic organ-

---

5. More abstractly, professionally certified knowledge on the research side holds the inputs constant, though this stretches the metaphor a bit too far.

izations. What needs to be explained, then, are the characteristic modes of coordination in higher education, which are described by Mintzberg's modes 5 and 1 (standardization of workers and mutual adjustment), in the light of the strong pull of professionalism.

This notion can be explored further by looking at the mutual adjustment and combining it with the second of the modes of coordination denoted by March and Simon—namely, "feedback." To complicate matters somewhat further, it must be noted (cf. Thompson, 1967; Van de Ven, Delbecq, & Koenig, 1976) that there are two forms of feedback: personal and group. In the first, individuals make adjustments in inputs and outputs as the need occurs to modify the interdepartmental connections. The individuals who do this are usually boundary personnel or executive personnel from each department. In the academic setting, for example, two faculty members from different departments may teach the same or similar courses and may be assigned the responsibility for coordinating their efforts.[6]

In addition to personal forms of feedback, there are group modes (Thompson, 1967, p. 56). In this configuration, the responsibility for mutual adjustment is given to a group of people—for example, a committee (either *ad hoc* or legislated). So, as Van de Ven, Delbecq, and Koenig (1976) note, there are really three modes of coordination in organizations: (1) programmed—impersonally, largely through bureaucratic means; (2) feedback—individual/personal; (3) and feedback—through groups. The issue raised by Van de Ven, Delbecq, and Koenig is what the organizational determinants of each mode are. What, in other words, determines when and where each kind of coordination will be found? The answers to this question are of considerable importance in helping to understand how decision making is carried out in colleges and universities. Indeed, "governance" may be seen not as a unique pattern of decision making but as a mode of integration that emerges as a response to certain organizational determinants.

Three organizational variables are proposed by Van de Ven, Delbecq, and Koenig to explain the likelihood of use of each mode of coordination: (1) task uncertainty; (2) interdependence; and (3) unit size. Their hypotheses are:

---

6. Once again, for reasons of space limitations, the example here is restricted to only one domain—transformation processes. Clearly, it would be of interest to consider coordination modes for decisions about inputs (personnel selection) and outputs (graduation standards).

1. The greater the task uncertainty, the more the tendency to use personal or group coordination methods. The reason is that with greater variability, more input from varied sources will contribute toward better solutions.
2. The greater the interdependence from pooled to sequential to reciprocal forms (Thompson, 1967), the more the organization tends to rely on group coordination methods.
3. The greater the size of the unit work force, the greater the use of impersonal, bureaucratic forms of coordination.

The first hypothesis can be illustrated with an example having to do with the advisement of graduate students. In the case of uncertainty about the direction of a student's dissertation, faculty committee members are likely to converse with one another interpersonally, either in dyads or as a committee. It is thus the uncertainty of the task that calls for the particular mode of coordination.

With respect to the second hypothesis, the authors suggest that the more dependent units are on one another, the more people must be engaged with one another to work out the necessary transactional and transitional problems between the units. For example, if it is determined that undergraduates need to have their curricular experiences in history and sociology coordinated (e.g, studying the history of the mid-nineteenth century and the sociology of Karl Marx at the same time), such coordination would not likely be effected through programmatic or bureaucratic coordination modes. Doubtless, there would be a faculty member from history and one from sociology collaborating in the effort, or each department would appoint members to a joint committee (cf. Tushman, 1979). As noted earlier, however, because of the domination of research objectives, informal cross-departmental communication is relatively rare.

The explanation of coordination modes through the use of the size variable (in the third hypothesis) is not as easily transferable to higher education. In contrast to the industrial sector, where control of large organizations can be managed through either centralization or decentralization (though, of course, neither is total), in colleges and universities an increase in size results in *simultaneous* centralization and decentralization (complicated or explained further by ownership — public versus private institutions). That is, the strain in academia is toward decentralization by product/service — the academic departments claiming the need to preserve their autonomy on the grounds of their unique, professional, disciplinary knowledge base and boundaries. As above, this claim is research driven and defended by differentiated intellectual paradigms and research methods. Since little interdependence is called for in research (i.e., there is little interdisciplinary or at least cross-departmental research), the design of the organization, however large, tends to accommodate these claims. In these circumstances, there is some question as to whether the hypothesized changes in coordination modes would change as departmental size increased.

The rather obvious point here is that in most universities such needs for frequent coordination for teaching functions either are not recognized or are ignored for political reasons. Hence, whatever coordination takes place will largely be ritualistic through extant committees or informal — for example, through chance meetings of faculty members, perhaps at lunches. More likely yet, it will be through the efforts of students to make connections among their courses (Bess, 1982, p. 81). Indeed, in the area of coordination of teaching, the primary mode of coordination is not any of those noted by Van de Ven, Delbecq, and Koenig, but by client integration — that is, by the student him/herself providing the necessary connections.

Van den Ven, Delbecq, and Koenig pursued these three hypotheses in an empirical research study of 197 units of a state employment security agency. Their findings are of interest and relevance. As they note:

> This research suggests that not only is there a *difference in degree of influence* of task uncertainty, task interdependence and work unit size on the use of coordination mechanisms in organizational units, there also appears to be a *difference in kind of influence* of each factor on the mechanisms of coordination used.
>
> As tasks increase in uncertainty, mutual work adjustments through horizontal communication channels and group meetings are used in lieu of coordination through hierarchy and impersonal programming. This *substitution* between alternative coordination mechanisms appears to be the major effect associated with task uncertainty. (emphasis in original) (1976, p. 332)

Perhaps most interesting among their conclusions is the notion that the use of hierarchical or bureaucratic channels for coordination purposes cannot be explained by the independent variables in their study. They suggest that "hierarchy is structurally pre-established, and it remains as the only stable mechanism of coordination, while the use of all other mechanisms varies under different unit conditions."

In other words, at least for the kinds of organizations in their study, the structure of decision making shifts according to task uncertainty, interdependence, and work unit size, but the bureaucratic hierarchy seems to remain, even if relatively less used in certain circumstances. There would seem to be important insights available from these findings for the understanding of institutions of higher education. Though the hierarchy of decision making in most complex colleges persists, the character of the coordination shifts according to other contingencies in the institution. That is, there are other antecedent conditions that predispose an academic organization to place more or less weight on the bureaucratic hierarchy. Since it is this most elusive, shifting, and ambiguous interstitial connection between the academic and nonacademic that has baffled researchers studying the organization of colleges and universities, it is important to search for and identify more precisely these antecedent conditions. As will be seen, they lie in part in the domain of politics in academia and in part in the strength of the two critical values of collegiality—trust and rationality. The political question is addressed in the next chapter, with collegiality following in Chapter 5.

CHAPTER

FOUR *Authority Structures and Power*

In earlier chapters, it was suggested that the modes of decision making in colleges and universities follow reasonably from the nature of the requirements for vertical and horizontal information flow. Information needs are themselves subject to the primary influences of environment, technology, and size (Pfeffer, 1978). "Perfectly" reasonable organizational design would lead to some optimum fit of structure to these various contingencies, thereby placing constraints on the achievement of the goals of individual members (Cyert & March, 1963). Under such conditions, we would expect universities to be designed to be readily adaptive to the many changes in their multiple constituencies, as well as optimally suited to the technologies of teaching and research.

The exact nature of those contingencies, as well as the manner in which they interact, however, is usually not clear to different individuals and subgroups within the organization. Limited perspectives and circumscribed rationality lead members of organizations, including colleges and universities, to suboptimize in order to maximize the likelihood of enhancing their own well-being (sometimes even at the cost of long-term organizational effectiveness, as contemporary critics of the current American business mentality tell us). Individuals seek power within and outside the organization to achieve personal goals. Despite efforts by institutional leaders to provide a unified focus, faculty, students, deans, department chairs, and president all view the good and welfare of the system quite naturally from their biased perspectives. As Pfeffer (1977) notes, "unless goals and criteria are shared among all participants in the organization, the use of power and influence is inevitable in organizational decision making."

There are, moreover, differential *opportunities* to achieve individual goals. These opportunities are distributed in nonrandom ways according to the power of individuals or groups.[1] Depending on the particular decision domain, power itself is influenced by the same contingencies (e.g., environment, technology, size, and information conditions) that dictate the organizational design, and in part by other factors (e.g., in the Hickson et al. [1971] strategic contingencies model). As Salancik and Pfeffer (1977) note, power is both an independent and a dependent variable. The acquisition of power by a dean, for example, is partly a function of the nature of the environment he/she faces or the technological requirements for mounting special programs or the availability of technical information to facilitate school goal achievement. The various tugs and pulls by the different subgroups to acquire and use power incline the institution to depart in varying degrees from the organizational design and authority structure that organizational efficiency would suggest. To some extent, the degree to which authority is dispersed in efficient ways (i.e., ways that serve to achieve alleged, *official*, organizational purposes) is also determined by the type of organization being considered. In some fields (e.g., industrial firms undergoing extremely rapid growth), authority appears to be highly irrationally dispersed, while in others (e.g., the military), it appears the opposite. Even within fields, however, there is considerable variance — as, for example, in higher education, where institutions from different sectors appear to have greater or lesser efficiency guiding their structures.

One way of illustrating the varied degrees of rationality[2] in a university's design is through the contingencies suggested by Pfeffer (1977). Using only two contingencies (in contrast with the several noted in the model in Figure 1.4), Pfeffer proposes to identify four different kinds of organizations. The two contingencies are (1) the amount of control possessed by authorities in the organization (Pfeffer is unclear about who "authorities" are, but it is assumed that he means those at the top of a pyramidal hierarchy); and (2) the degree of agreement of the members as to organizational goals and the

---

1. While group or subunit power is intimately associated with individual power (e.g., see, Beyer, 1982), only the latter is discussed here.

2. The words "rational" and "efficient" are used interchangeably here, both implying the application of intelligence to the solution of organizational problems without regard to the impacts on those making the decisions. This is not to be confused with Simon's description of rationality — more properly, limited rationality — which is concerned with the constraints on individuals resulting from information shortages and ambiguities.

technology to achieve them. (Pfeffer's joining of the variables of goals and technology is somewhat problematic, as is the absence of the contingencies of environment and size; but Pfeffer might argue that these latter are themselves contingent on the two he suggests.)

Thus, as Pfeffer (1977) observes, organizations can be arrayed in four quadrants depending on these two variables (Figure 4.1). What is suggested in the Pfeffer model is that under conditions of low control by centralized authorities, decisions tend to be dominated by informal "processes," while for organizations where control of authorities is high, formal, "structural" characteristics of the organization can better explain the decision-making process. This process/structure issue undergirds much of the analysis of academic organizations that appears in the literature. Indeed, it is relatively easy to recast the predominant models of college and university organization outlined in Chapter 1 into this matrix, omitting, for the moment, the centralized model, which applies to relatively few colleges. Since as Mintzberg (1979, p. 358; cf. Schriesheim, Von Glinow & Kerr, 1977) notes, professionals in organizations tend not only to resist traditional bureaucracies but to "seek collective control of the administrative decisions that affect them," it would appear that faculty will lean toward the left-hand side of the matrix, while administrations will seek to establish the patterns on the right. For various reasons, not the least of which is the obligations that accompany power, neither side will want an organization that is overwhelmingly

Figure 4.1
Models of Organization Based
on Control and Goal/Technology Consensus

	Amount of Control Possessed by Organizational Authorities	
	LOW	HIGH
Consensus About Goals/ Technology (Certainty)	Professional Model (1)	Bureaucratic Model (2)
Dissensus About Goals/ Technology (Uncertainty)	Political/ Coalition Model (3)	Centralized Model (4)

Adapted from Pfeffer (1977, p. 240).

favorable to its interests, but each will want an edge in crucial decision making. Variations will occur, of course, depending on the degree of institutional differentiation, with community colleges tending to be closer to the right and highly research-oriented universities to the left.

Most institutions of higher education, then, seem to be structured in varying degrees to accommodate the needs of professionals for participation (or at least enfranchisement) in decisions that affect the organizational tasks they perform. As will be discussed in Chapter 5, collegiality (more specifically, "s-collegiality") has come to be associated with such decision-making prerogatives.

Unfortunately, the axes in the Pfeffer model do not adequately explain the distribution of institutions of higher learning that fall into each of the four boxes, nor do they explain the "shape" of the decision-making structures that characterize the four models. That is, consensus on goals and technology and amount of control held by central authorities are derivatives — manifestations of a more fundamental set of contingencies that more clearly explain the particular structures for decision making that develop in different institutions. Since a primary objective of this book is to explain those structures, it is necessary to seek additional means. The discussion returns next, therefore, to a consideration of the influences on a university that incline it toward efficient operation.

Two kinds of "influences" can be found in the typical academic structure, each acting to constrain decision makers to behave in certain ways. These are, on the one hand, the norms of trust and of belief in rationality that are embedded in the culture and that may lead in varying degrees to collegial structure and processes. These induce action in the direction of logical, unbiased decisions intended to forward efficiently organizational objectives perceived to be held in common, and away from disproportionate personal gain at the expense of organizational efficiency. In an "efficient" organization, these forces, which take the form of the norms, values, and attitudes that obtain in the dominant culture of the organization, complement formal, official policies and constrain behavior in the direction of organizational ends (see Zand, 1974, 1981, on the "collateral organization"; also, Stein & Kanter, 1980, on the "parallel" organization). Further, confidence in the system's capacity for distributive justice (equity in individual benefits) encourages participants to believe that through their efforts, there will be a happy coincidence of achievement of organizational and personal goals (cf. Gamson, 1968). Personal effort, in other words, results under these conditions in organizational well-being, which in turn redounds to individual benefits shared equitably.

On the other hand, irrational influences force decisions and organizational design away from rationality and toward different objectives that are seen to be held by separate individuals or groups and that may not be common to all. Says Pettigrew, "As long as organizations continue as resource-sharing systems where there is an inevitable scarcity of those resources, political behavior will occur" (1973, p. 20; cf. Tushman & Nadler, 1980). In organizations where the dominant coalition has failed either to convince others of the "rationality" of the system and hence the equity of the existing distribution of benefits, or has been unable to "cool them out," the culture and norms of the organization will not generally be supportive of most organizational objectives—high organizational achievement and high individual satisfaction and motivation (cf. Scott, Mitchell, & Birnbaum, 1981, pp. 304–305). Excessive amounts of energy spent by lower participants to influence the dominant coalition will drain away energy that could otherwise be more productively oriented. Colleges and universities rife with politics, in other words, may appear to be effective but are not efficient in either the usual sense of that term or in Barnard's (1938) meaning. Though an institution may seem to be producing at high quality, the well-known hidden costs of politics reduce the commitment of faculty and/or administrators and direct their energy to self-serving behaviors intended primarily to redress perceived imbalances in the distribution of benefits.

Thus, irrational influences take the form of political activity (cf. Robbins, 1983). They result in authority being vested inefficiently from an organizational perspective, resulting in wasted resources and a disproportionate ratio of resources to contributions. Regardless of the degree to which organizational goals are shared, political activity may be irrational. Again, authority is vested inefficiently, and benefits are distributed out of proportion to contributions to the organization. In both cases—that is, when goals are shared or are disparate—power drives organizations to irrational modes of dealing with the two key determinants of structure discussed earlier, namely, information needs (Galbraith) and task uncertainty and interdependence (Van de Ven, Delbecq, & Koenig).

This discussion reflects the suggestion made earlier that the culture of a university is drawn in either of two directions—toward rationality and trust (discussed further in the following chapter), leading to collegiality, or toward irrationality and distrust, giving the institution a political orientation. In sum, instead of two decision-making structures on a continuum from collegial to bureaucratic, with politics intervening in both, as in the Childers (1981) model, it is more reasonable to postulate only one structure, with two forces, rationality and irrationality, each exerting influences. The "structure" is thus an administrative apparatus for decision making that has characteristics of both collegiality and bureaucracy (see Becker & Gordon, 1964; Eastcott, 1977). Of interest is the degree to which the structure is informally bent toward rationality or toward politics — the extent to which culture and leadership incline faculty and administrators to use universalistic vs. particularistic judgments in their decisions. This is not, of course, to say that there is not variance in decision-making structures across institutions, particularly across different types of institutions. It is only to note that the structures themselves are more influenced by other contingencies, while the *use* of the structures can best be comprehended by the forces noted in Figure 1.4. These are the same two opposing forces — the Dionysian and Apollonian — that have been recognized since the time of the Greeks as inherent in all forms of organization (biological, personal, social, and cultural — cf. Parsons & Platt, 1973). So there is good reason to believe that they continue to inhere in formal organizational settings.

The question, then, is how and why these two critical influences affect the distribution of authority over the four critical domains (inputs, transformation processes, outputs, and feedback) of important decisions in colleges and universities.

Power and Politics in Organizations

Earlier chapters contained discussions of the manner in which information constrains the determination of organizational structure and, importantly, the concomitant dependencies that structure the power relationships. Also considered were the needs for coordination and the resultant power configurations. It is necessary now to turn more directly to the concept of power in organizations, particularly colleges and universities, to identify the reasons power affects information control and flow as well as organizational structure and coordination mechanisms. The suggestion was made in Chapter 1 that the structures and processes embodied in academic governance could be explained using the logic of organizational analysis. Here, then, the focus is on the deviations from or violations of the order of rationality.

The first part of this section consists of a brief review of the literature on this subject, preparatory to applying some of the concepts to organizations of higher education.[3] A conceptual model of the political process will first be presented. It will then be applied to each of the four domains of activity delineated above in order to clarify how authority over each is distributed across the structure of administration in most colleges and universities.

Hrebiniak (1978; cf. Georgiou, 1973; Zand, 1981) suggests that if organizations are conceived of as "marketplaces," the arena for the manifestations of the above alternative power modes becomes clearer.

> Within the marketplace, contributions are assessed with respect to how easily they can be replaced—i.e., their importance to others in the organization. Individuals who provide services that others see as critical also receive inducements reflecting their contributions. Thus, they receive more than others, which necessarily leads to an uneven distribution and control of resources. (Hrebiniak, 1978, p. 178)

Hrebiniak goes on to say that internal dependencies create power differentials, with the less dependent unit having more power, especially if its services are essential to organizational well-being. Further, perceptions of inequality in power distribution must be sanctioned by the members of the organization, at least in the short run. That is, recognition and acceptance of power are required for the organization to function. This is not to say, of course, that attempts to redress the power imbalance do not take place contemporaneously with its acceptance. The "outs" strive always to be "ins" (Blau, 1964). Since power enables organizational members to change the directions and structures of the organization, those out of power seek it in

---

3. Given the proliferation of writing in recent years on the subject of politics, this book can obviously do no more than touch on the key pieces in the literature. For the interested reader, in addition to the citations noted in the text, the following are of more immediate relevance to the topic. First, the "strategic contingencies approach" (Hickson, Hinings, Lee, Schneck, & Pennings, 1971; Hinings, Hickson, Pennings, & Schneck, 1974; Salancik & Pfeffer, 1977; Miles, 1980, pp. 151 ff). Second, coalitional models (Cyert & March, 1963; Mintzberg, 1984). Third, resource dependencies models (Beyer, 1982). Fourth, structural models (Kanter, 1979; Hrebiniak, 1978, pp. 173 ff). Last, interpersonal exchange models (French & Raven, 1959; Bacharach & Lawler, 1980).

order to further their own interests. Indeed, as Bacharach and Lawler (1980, p. 25) note, "Power potential, power use, and the consequences of power potential or power use are distinct phenomena and must be treated as such on both a theoretical and empirical level."

Who acquires power is a function of the nature of the environmental contingencies seen as important to the organization, the technologies of the transformation processes, and the size of the organization. The organization as a whole and subparts of it develop critical dependencies (and individuals work to create images of dependencies) that must be managed if the organization is to survive and be successful. As Pfeffer (1978, p. 126) notes, "the critical question for assessing the structural consequence of dependence is where in the organization the capability for dealing with the dependence resides."

Where environments are turbulent and complex, for example, boundary spanning units or personnel will become more important. Thus, in times of uncertain fluctuations in student demand and in funding, personnel concerned with these issues appear more prominently. On the other hand, where transformation processes are seen to be intangible and ineffable, personnel who perform those transformations will be viewed as critical resources and will, accordingly, acquire power. For example, teachers come to be seen as powerful in institutions where the quality of the student output is highly valued. As still another illustration, where information flow is critical to organizational functioning (e.g., when new accounting or student information or tracking systems are implemented), those in control of information production and the channels of information distribution will come to be seen as powerful. And when size requires the imposition of vertical hierarchies for coordination purposes, those seen as controlling final decisions will be viewed as powerful. As Pfeffer (1981, p. 98) notes, "The power of organizational actors is fundamentally determined by two things, the importance of what they do in the organization and their skill in doing it."

Some of these notions have been validated empirically by Hickson et al. (1971). Their findings are that power is related to three variables: uncertainty, substitutability, and centrality. In Hrebiniak's words:

> The greater the centrality and ability to cope with uncertainty, and the less the substitutability, the greater is the likelihood of a role or unit's having power. (1978, p. 177)

Thus far, the word "power" has been used somewhat loosely. It is necessary now to be more precise in order better to see how it is employed in colleges and universities. The extensive literature on the subject yields many definitions, but the distinctions made by Bacharach and Lawler (1980) seem appropriate to this setting. They suggest that one must understand the differences among "sources," "types," and "bases" of power in organizations.

Sources of power reflect the recourse to which power holders appeal when power is exercised. Bacharach and Lawler indicate four separate sources: (1) office or structural position; (2) personal characteristics; (3) expertise; and (4) opportunity (primarily the informal side of organizations—the submerged part of the organizational iceberg).

By *type* of power, Bacharach and Lawler mean either legitimate power (i.e., authority) or influence. "Authority," they argue, "is zero-sum in nature: a party either does or does not have the right to make the final decisions in a given context; if one party has the right, another does not have it." On the other hand, influence can vary in organizations depending on conditions of structure and technology. The fact that one person or group has influence does not necessarily mean that another does not. This distinction between authority and influence is important to bear in mind in considering how decisions are made in colleges and universities (cf. Parsons & Platt, 1973). For example, while most research on decision making in these institutions looks to ultimate sources of authority ("who has the final veto power?"), few identify the influences on the decision makers who have authority. Also important to bear in mind is that in most academic organizations, not all important decisions are referred to formal authorities. Many academic decisions, especially in small work groups, are made by mutual agreement. It is only when conflict within or between groups occurs that the source of "authority" is invoked for adjudication purposes. In still other words, decisions in colleges and universities are frequently made on the basis of the exercise of influence, with authority held in reserve. As noted earlier (cf. Van de Ven & Delbecq, 1974), the authority structure of the bureaucracy remains as an adjudicatory force.

Finally, *bases* of power, in the Bacharach and Lawler schema, refer to the sanctions that are available to power holders as they exercise either authority or influence. Several bases of power are available, depending on source and type: coercion, remuneration, informal norms, and knowledge. Arrayed in tabular form, the relationships are shown in Figure 4.2.

**Figure 4.2
An Analysis of Power**

SOURCE	TYPE	BASES
Structure	Authority	Coercion Remunerative Normative Knowledge
Personality	Influence	Normative Knowledge
Expertise	Influence	Normative Knowledge
Opportunity	Influence	Coercion Knowledge

Adapted from Bacharach and Lawler (1980, p. 36).

From the figure, it can be seen that authority stems from organizational structure and that those who have authority have available as bases of power all four modes — coercion, remuneration, norms, and knowledge. Note that in this conceptualization power is seen as both contextual and process-related — and must be understood using both frameworks (cf. Thompson & Luthans, 1983). It is exercised through distant and proximate interactions. For example, individuals whose power source is in the organizational structure draw that power through their ability to provide resources (i.e., through budgetary allocations and/or salary dispensations), through the management of uncertainty (i.e., the control of critical knowledge), and through the manipulation of consensus and norms (cf. Pfeffer, 1981, pp. 99ff). (In colleges and universities coercion rarely will be employed — cf. Etzioni, 1961.) On the other hand, power holders having sources in personality (rather than organizational structure) can also exercise influence through the manipulation of norms or through the giving or withholding of knowledge. Charismatic faculty wield their power, in other words, through their ability to establish normative directions or constraints on faculty and administrator actions or by their sharing of needed knowledge.

One further aspect of the Bacharach and Lawler theory needs to be outlined here. The above represents power largely as held and manifested by *individuals* in organizations. The model has special explanatory cogency in large, research-oriented universities. In these types of institutions, decentralization is extensive. As noted earlier (in the discussion above of Helsabeck), not only do faculty participate more fully in all kinds of decisions that are judged to be professional, but each faculty member tends to be seen as an autonomous worker, with little interdependence in the collectivity. In these circumstances, the analysis of personal rather than subunit power reveals much about the nature of the enterprise.

Personal power in the Bacharach and Lawler model is exercised as influence and derives its sources from the personality, expertise, and opportunity seen by individual faculty members. A variety of modes of exercising personal influence have been identified in the literature (see, e.g., Kipnis, Schmidt, & Wilkinson, 1980; Falbo, 1977). One mode of particular relevance here was suggested by MacMillan (1978; see also the antecedent and quite similar list of Gamson, 1968). *Power* according to MacMillan is the capacity of an actor to structure situations in ways that constrain another to act in ways favorable to the actor. The primary mode for accomplishing this is to restructure the other's *perceptions* so as to get him or her to act in desired directions. Four means of restructuring perceptions are possible:

1. Inducement — changing the situation so that the other perceives that his circumstances are improved by complying.
2. Coercion — changing the situation so that the other perceives the circumstances are aggravated by noncompliance.
3. Persuasion — changing the perception, rather than the situation, so that the other reconceives of the proposed activity as having positive benefits.
4. Obligation — calling attention to the value/implications of alternative actions so that the other sees the obligation to act in the proposed way, even if he/she fares worse as a result.

The obvious and heavy reliance on "cognitive rationality" (Parsons & Platt, 1973) in these methods renders them especially useful in understanding academic decision making. For example, one can readily understand the dynamics of faculty member–dean relationships as built not only on accumulated power in Pfeffer's terms (e.g., grounded in control over resources or information), but on the modes of exercising power noted by MacMillan. In still other words, one must explain power relationships both structurally and processually. On the other hand, the relative insularity of faculty labor, both in research and teaching, renders the influence side of faculty power less potent than the authority side of administrative power. That is, in the Bacharach and Lawler scheme, the "type" of power in a confrontation is critical. In these cases, faculty in research institutions often find it necessary to form alliances outside of the formal decision-making structure. Understanding the nature of "coalitions" and coalition formation is thus important in understanding how power is exercised.[4]

According to Bacharach and Lawler,[5] "Coalitions are the mechanisms that crystallize and bring conflicting interests to the foreground, while intercoalition bargaining is the process through which organizational members act on and deal with their conflicting interests" (p. 138). A coalition is also "a dense clustering of reciprocal relationships within any network" (p. 205). Further, the bargaining that goes on between coalitions is determined in part by the nature and extent of the dependency relationships among the parties. Bacharach and Lawler suggest that in more structurally complex and heterogeneous organizations, there will be more coalitions, few identified as having large domains of influence and each exhibiting relatively little overlap between the influence network and the formal authority structure (p. 207). Thus, in large universities, a diversity of faculty coalitions may be anticipated, each relatively independent from the administration (including both the academic and administrative sides), with each attempting to wield influence to forward its own interests.[6] For example, it is reasonable to expect to find informal groups of faculty members who are not part of the senate or

---

4. Indeed, the word "coalition" connotes a system of opposed political forces and may not be entirely accurate in this context. At any rate, in collegial systems, the dominant coalition is a broadly based one.

5. For a different approach, see the conceptualization of Mintzberg (1983, pp. 306–307) describing the alleged exhaustive set of coalition possibilities.

6. It was noted above that coalitions attempt to maximize their own interests, even if those interests may be at odds with others. There are, however, constraints on their ability to do this. Thompson (1967, p. 133) reiterates the March and Simon (1958) observation that control by coalitions is usually achieved through the specification of "decision premises" of other members' "(1) beliefs about cause/effect relations and (2) preferences regarding possible outcomes." The power of a dominant coalition to place constraints on the cause/effect premises of others is vitiated by three contingencies: incompleteness of knowledge; client variability and resistance; and competing inducements or threats. Constraints on control of outcome preferences of others are attributed to the strength of the participants' own beliefs and the ability of the organization to secure sufficient inputs to achieve the preferred outcomes.

senate committee structure united in goals and strategies (though not explicitly through written documents) in the pursuit of their goals — for example, lighter teaching loads.

The influence of these groups is, of course, countered by a corresponding effort at control by those in positions of authority (Gamson, 1968). As noted in the Introduction, what has been called "loose coupling" or even "organized anarchy" in educational institutions may be an illusory phenomenon, occasioned by the relative subtlety of influence relations in such organizations and by the difficulty of identifying them through the more traditional, positivist research methods.

A quite different approach to understanding power is necessary in institutions with exclusively teaching missions. Here, individuals (faculty) without formal roles in the administrative structure, and generally without recourse to any of the modes for accessing power, lack personal power. In more centralized organizations, there will be fewer coalitions (see Tonn, 1978), and power is more frequently exercised through structural sources via the authority "type" (in the Bacharach and Lawler model). In community colleges, for example, coalition formation will be more restricted, as faculty members are more rigidly bound to the formal role requirements specified in the procedures manuals established by the formal hierarchy. In contrast to universities, where loose job descriptions and much job variety permit confederations around faculty-generated interests, in community colleges (and other more administratively dominated colleges) single-function professionals (cf. Charns, Lawrence, & Weisbord, 1977) are more likely to see their interests forwarded through formal departmental structures, if not through interest groups such as unions.

It is possible now to attempt to relate these conceptualizations of power to the earlier discussion of rationality vs. politics as influencing forces governing the decision-making structure of colleges and universities. Above, it was noted that universities typically fall into the two quadrants (in Figure 4.1) that Pfeffer conceptualized as "low control by organizational authorities," while community colleges are more likely to appear in the "high control" sectors. For universities in the "professional" sector, relations among organizational participants are conditioned by consensus on goals and the technology to achieve them. In the other sector in which universities might fall (political/coalition model) there is dissensus on both counts. In the first type, the predominant influence is professional in character; in the second, it is political/coalitional or "nonrational." It is important to note that influence processes, including coalition formation, take place in all four of the types of organizations in the Pfeffer model. There are, however, differences not only in the amount of coalition formation but in their goals and instruments of activity. For example, in Pfeffer's professional-type organizations, the activities of the coalitions in their efforts to gain advantages for themselves fall into a more "analytic" mode, while for political organizations, there is more "bargaining" (see March & Simon, 1958, for a discussion of the differences between these two). In negotiations, formal and informal, in professional organizations there is an assumption that differences can be resolved through problem solving or persuasion. All parties can be presumed to benefit from creative solutions, since goals are held in common. Indeed, even in more bureaucratic organizations like community colleges, Weberian theory suggests a high consensus on goals, thus eliminating (again, in theory) the need for partisan politicking.

In the political organization, on the other hand (and, to some extent, in the centralized organization — lower right in the Pfeffer table), the assumption is made that the "game" is a zero-sum one, such that the participants find it necessary to maximize their own advantage to the detriment of the others. "Bargaining," as a tactic of coalitions, thus involves a variety of power devices, including some that are subversive and/or immoral. They involve the formation of alliances both within and outside of the system or subsystem of affiliation. To some extent, this is mitigated by the overarching norms of professional conduct and the local norms of academic etiquette that commonly prevail. As Pfeffer (1981, p. 156) notes, "For the moment we assert that the myth of organizational goals serves to transform the decision situation into somewhat less of a zero-sum game than what typically is faced in the arena of legislative politics or experimental games."

There have been many empirical studies or perceptions of decision-making power in colleges and universities (e.g., Beyer & Lodahl, 1976). A recent one (Carnegie Foundation for the Advancement of Teaching, 1982) identified 39 key decisions in three areas — academic, personnel, and administration — and revealed how respondents in various constituencies on and off campuses perceived for each of the decisions the locus of "effective authority" across 12 possible authority holders (e.g., departments, faculty senate, campus administration, governing board). While the "perception" of power is an organizational question of importance (cf. Lindquist & Blackburn, 1974; Pfeffer, 1981, Ch. 2; Kenen & Kenen, 1978), the question of concern here is with the identification and understanding of the distribution of real power and authority.

To this point, the focus has been on the political dimensions that may affect how authority is distributed. In the next chapter, the constraints on politics that may stem from the culture of collegiality are considered. In that chapter, the forms of organizational structure that may prevail depending on the play of politics, beliefs in efficiency, and trust in others will be arrayed.

CHAPTER

FIVE *Authority Structures and Collegiality*

In most societies, there is a cycle of alternating emphases on control and freedom for citizens. After particularly permissive periods, societies frequently seek to impose tighter restrictions on individuals. Sometimes these may be found to be too binding and are followed by the granting of more individual freedom. So also in organizations, especially those staffed by professionals, there is a strain between freedom and control, perceived by workers as more or less stressful depending on the degree of worker involvement in the organization and on membership in its dominant coalition. As the pendulum swings, workers see varying phases, ranging from greater amounts of hierarchical authority to considerable amounts of freedom, with the interim stages perceived as moderately supportive or unsupportive. Almost invariably, however, there is a sense of ambiguity regarding the nature and strength of power and authority over the various domains of decision making, with different kinds of ambiguity depending on the direction that the pendulum is swinging. While it has some positive value, this flux is the source of some confusion and conflict as workers seek to make policy and carry out directives. It is manifested behaviorally as expressed confusion and conflict over the particulars of these directives, as well as the authority to issue them.

Colleges and universities as organizations suffer (or benefit) from these same shifting modalities in organizational control style and policy. Faculty and administrators are frequently faced with unspecified and changing degrees of freedom regarding their authority in academic and nonacademic decisions. For example, a president in one era may find no resistance to his or her establishing a student dormitory curfew or a salary ceiling on faculty compensation, while a decade later, a successor president may be unable to issue a policy directive on who may park where. In earlier chapters, some solutions to this uncertainty were explained in terms of the information-handling structures that emerge. In this chapter, another explanation is introduced—this time bridging the cultural, structural, and processual domains. "Collegiality," despite its frequent use in the language of governance, is a relatively unexplored concept, certainly little understood in terms of standard organizational theory. Since the claim is frequently made that collegiality is critical to organizational effectiveness in higher education, it is important that educational leaders have more precise notions of the concept and the phenomena to which it refers. It is the purpose of this chapter to help clarify the nature of collegiality, to show its varied uses, and to identify the institutional pathologies that may arise from misunderstandings of its nature. More particularly, what is explored is the strength of collegiality as an important force in determining the nature of decision making in higher education. As before, the purpose is to unveil the mystique of the concept, using common terms from the organizational theory literature.

A brief word is necessary first about the method of this chapter. Whereas most social scientists observe phenomena, label them, and describe their relation to other phenomena, here there is already a label given to what many people believe are commonly held behavioral referents. That is, the academic community has adopted some usages of the term "collegiality," which it assumes refer to some agreed-upon phenomena. In this chapter, however, the procedure will be to characterize some phenomena that *could* be assumed to be collegial, recognizing that by some definitions they may not be. The intention, in other words, is not so much to find a set of phenomena that all would agree are collegial as to locate some organizational phenomena that serve some useful and/or harmful functions so that the phenomena can be manipulated as necessary. The label "collegiality" is thus a heuristic to the inquiry, not an absolute constraint on what must be described.

Collegiality consists of three distinct components, two of which are relatively static, the other dynamic. The first is *culture* (or normative framework); the second, decision-making *structure*; and the third, the process of *behaving*, which is constrained by the first two. As a culture, collegiality comprises an unevenly distributed set of beliefs about what is appropriate behavior in the organization; as a decision-making structure, collegiality is a formal, manifested set of organizational rules for decisions to be made (which, in other circumstances, would either fall ambiguously in the interstices of bureaucracy or be handled through bureaucratic modes likely to be perceived as illegitimate); and as a process, collegiality is a behavior set governing individual action and interaction among faculty and between faculty and administrators, and is guided by both culture and structure. The behaviors in the interactions are usually characterized by tolerance of, deference to, or even collaboration with those holding alien positions.

The behavioral science language describing collegiality typically borrows from several idioms. At the cultural level, invocations of broad, liberal, and humanistic values for entire systems or institutions are found. At the structural level, the parlance of politics and civil or parliamentary democracy is the mode of discourse, while in interpersonal behaviors, the language partakes more of social psychology, particularly interpersonal and group dynamics. While these three dimensions—culture, structure, and behavior—are familiar concepts in organizational theory used to explain the actions of participants in organizations in the profit-making sector, their unique admixture in the higher education setting has not been adequately considered.

It is proposed further that the idea of collegiality "inhabits" each of these domains via two quintessential values and their corollaries that are central to all organizations, but especially to institutions of higher education. Both have to do with the strength of worker beliefs in the benignancy of two resources on which organizational members depend—the system itself and co-workers. In other words, collegiality refers to: (1) the belief in the propriety of order and rationality in the structure and process of deliberations concerning organizational decisions; and (2) the belief in and commitment to the value of "trust" in other organizational workers. In more professional organizations, which are self-governing, there is an overlap between these belief sets.

More particularly, collegiality as an idea invades the three domains—again, culture, structure, and behavior—by virtue of the power of these values. The strength of collegiality in different institutions can be measured by considering the magnitudes of the values and their manifestations—that is, the belief and action patterns that characterize the college or university. The beliefs may vary from strong to weak, and the actions from frequent to infrequent. The two beliefs—structured rationality and interpersonal trust—and their corollaries are listed below:

1. Belief in rationality and order—the extent to which problems are seen as being satisfactorily resolved through concerted decision making according to existing organizational repertories.
   a. Information flow—satisfactions with the nature and amount of information exchange through the organization, particularly about when and how much information to share with whom (see Chapter 2).
   b. Coordination—satisfactions with the modes of resolution of inter-unit and interpersonal conflicts over work matters (see Chapter 3).
2. Trust—the strength of belief in the goodness of others and the willingness to act on that belief (see Chapter 4).
   a. Individual/organizational balance—satisfactions with the relative emphases on the achievement of individual and organizational goals.
   b. Self/other balance—satisfactions with the weights placed on cooperative and competitive effort (or the degree to which ego is invested in other).

Depending on the strength of these primary dimensions, organizations tend to move into five prototypical configurations: anarchy/polity, bureaucracy, oligarchy, clan/family, and collegium. These configurations are familiar (see, for example, Pfeffer, 1977; Baldridge et al., 1978). In Figure 5.1, these configurations are displayed in a two-dimensional matrix, the axes of which are the powerful explanatory variables of rationality and trust noted above.

In order to understand these types of organizations, the nature of rationality and trust in organizations is discussed first, followed by a consideration of the degree of their presence or absence in the three domains—organizational culture, organizational structure, and organizational behavior. The interaction of these themes is then considered in a discussion of the functions of collegiality for colleges and universities.

Beliefs Underpinning Collegiality

As noted above, there are two key beliefs that underlie conceptualizations of collegiality and the ways in which it is manifested: (1) the value attached to the belief in rationality and order as a mode of decision making; and (2) the value of trust as organizationally utilitarian and ultimately self-serving. What is meant by rationality here

Figure 5.1
S-Collegiality as a Function
of Trust and Rationality

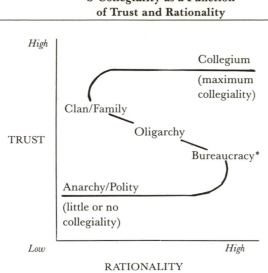

*In Weber's highly cognitive conception of bureaucracy, of course, trust is not a consideration, since it was assumed that the hierarchy of authority was established through rational judgments of task competence. Here, a more twentieth-century and perhaps Marxian view of bureaucracies is taken, in recognition of the likelihood that some degree of alienation (and hence distrust) between management and workers exists. These categories (management and workers), however, are spread ambiguously across faculty and administration in higher education, which may, in fact, be part of one cause of the distrust.

is related to but not the same as the "cognitive rationality" to which Parsons and Platt give much attention. The latter suggest that rationality in the American University is:

> a mode of action institutionalized in social systems. Rationality is characterized by conformity with cognitive norms and values wherever such conformity is relevant. The individual is conceived to act rationally "in social roles" where expectations are structured in favor of cognitive criteria and where conformity with such expectations will be rewarded. (1973, p. 80)

Whereas Parsons and Platt conceive of cognitive rationality as an interpenetration of cultural and social systems surrounding the primacy of "knowledge" as a basis for intelligent action, here a different meaning is given to rationality, since the concern here is primarily with actions that require decisions having implications that are more organizational than individual.[1] That is, Parsons and Platt see knowledge as driving professors, particularly research-oriented professors, toward actions that are rational to the degree that they are grounded in fact and reason, not opinion — a tradition that originated in universities after the revolution of science and empiricism in the seventeenth and eighteenth centuries. However, decisions that may have impacts on others in the organization may, it is suggested here, be driven by factors other than the Parsons and Platt notion of cognitive rationality — namely, the belief in the rationality of the design and operation of the organizational structure. The strength of that belief, following this argument, is what we usually mean by "collegiality." That is, a system is said to be collegial if there is belief in the rationality of its decision-making system. This is not, of course, to suggest that knowledge is irrelevant to organizational decisions in higher education. It is only to imply that academics believe that when a system is rationally designed, knowledge can be most effectively utilized and, perhaps more important, will be. Bias and opinion will be less likely to interfere with sound decision making in a rational system.

Belief in the rationality of the system is one part of what is commonly associated with collegiality. It guides, in part, the way in which faculty relate to one another. Indeed, as meanings attached by faculty to knowledge of one kind or another tend to be diversified by discipline, if not by individual, in more collegial institutions faith in the decision-making structure is substituted for insistence on complete knowledge. In a collegial organization faculty *must* believe in the system because they cannot be privy to all knowledge required for decisions. "Limited rationality" (Simon, 1957) encourages not only more bureaucracy, but, in a collegial system, more faith in the decision-making structure. To be sure, cognition based on knowledge forms the groundwork of decision making, but no more so in universities than in the nonprofit sector.

What is meant here is closer to the Weberian notion of the legitimacy of bureaucratic decision making, except that instead of a patrimonial or hierarchical bureaucracy, the structure is collegial. Weber saw rational social (e.g., organizational) action as being manifested in two modes: *zweckrational* and *wertrational* (Weber, 1947, p. 115).

---

1. For a useful discussion of alternative conceptions of "rationality," see Diesing, 1962.

These correspond essentially to action taken to forward one's own individual ends according to a calculation of the instrumentality of other objects and persons as serving those ends and action taken in obeisance to some cause, regardless of the personal consequences. Collegiality embodies both of these notions, as participants in collegial organizational decision making believe both in the idea of collegiality and in the efficacy of the system to attend to their individual aims. As Weber noted, rational/legal authority, when accepted, incorporates the force of ideology to ensure compliance with organizational directives. (Weber, of course, denied the possibility of "democracy" in a bureaucratic setting, because of the short-term nature of political office and the lack of required expertise on the part of those in power. See Gerth & Mills, 1946, p. 226; Satow, 1975; Staw, 1980.)

The definition here includes the differentiation made by Scott, Mitchell, and Peery (1981) in which rationality means not only the perceived reasonableness of the system to accomplish organizational objectives of efficiency and coordination, but its correctness as a political statement that will attend to individual needs for equity and justice. It also includes what Gamson (1968) calls political trust in the institutions of a regime, though we do not refer here to trust in Gamson's other three objects: incumbent authorities, public philosophy, or political community.

To sum up, belief in rationality in colleges and universities is the degree to which members of an academic community place their faith in the decision-making structure as a satisfactory mechanism for attending to the organization's problems as well as their own needs. The spin-offs or corollaries of this belief in rationality may be seen in the nature of information-sharing and coordination mechanisms, as noted in earlier chapters. In a system with strong beliefs in rationality, information is readily and widely shared throughout the organization, thus mitigating the need for investments in vertical systems or the creation of lateral relations. Further, by virtue of the imputed inherent rationality of the system, workers tend to see roles as being played by those with competence. That is, just as Weber conceived of bureaucracies as a hierarchically structured set of roles, with skills and talents the basis of placement of people in the hierarchy, so also in a college or university setting dominated by collegiality, the organizational structure is perceived to be staffed with workers competent to do their jobs. Following from this are assumptions that most workers are motivated to work hard and that close supervision is therefore unnecessary. The obverse is true in noncollegial institutions.

The second ingredient in the definition of collegiality noted above is trust. Whereas for rationality, belief is centered in the efficacy of the organization viewed nomothetically as a system of depersonalized roles and role relationships, trust, in contrast, involves beliefs in human beings (considered both universalistically and particularistically; cf. Hoy & Kupersmith, 1984; Zucker, 1986). The first corollary to trust is the balance of weight placed on the achievement of individual and organizational goals. In a highly collegiate system, the belief is that there is no necessary conflict between individual and organizational goals. It is presumed that the system *per se* is neither inherently malevolent nor exploitive of individuals in the interests of attaining organizational goals. Indeed, the system best succeeds by virtue of the achievement of individual goals, which are coincident with those of the organization. Further, the distribution of benefits for work performed (the inducements/contributions balance) is seen to be roughly equitable. Hence, trust in others is a valid and functional belief, since the system is seen as a collection of individuals pursuing compatible goals (cf. Durkheim, 1933).

The second corollary to trust is the belief that there is no necessary conflict among individual goals. As above, the achievement of individual goals is perceived to benefit all. Conflict resolution in a highly collegiate system, then, tends to be collaborative, focusing on the integrative rather than the distributive dimension (Thomas, 1976). That is, the emphasis is on finding ways to increase the "size of the pie," rather than on how a "fixed size pie" should be cut up.

With these notions of the essential belief structure of collegiality in mind, it is possible to turn to the three levels of organizational life where they are manifested — organizational culture, structure, and behavior.

The Culture of Collegiality

This discussion can best begin by identifying the concept of culture as "ideational." That is, culture exists not in physical, palpable form, but as a collection of ideas about behavior that exist in the minds of organizational workers.[2] Sometimes, the ideas are quite clear; at

---

2. Note that this is a very different concept from some other perspectives on culture (e.g., Van Maanen & Barley, 1985; Schein, 1985), which view culture as a combination of artifacts, structure, process, and value. While this interactionist orientation has considerable validity (particularly recognizing the inextricable na-

other times, they are amorphous. Aggregated across workers, the ideas serve partially to guide behavior. Depending on several contingencies, workers adhere in varying degrees to the guides. The concept of culture as employed in this book shares Payne's definition of "organizational climate":

> a molar concept reflecting the content and strength of prevalent values, norms, attitudes, behaviors, and feelings of the members of a social system. (1971)

Further, from Deal and Kennedy, the corporate culture comprises values:

> These are the basic concepts and beliefs of an organization; as such they form the heart of the corporate culture. Values define "success" in concrete terms for employees — "if you do this, you too will be a success" — and establish standards of achievement within the organization. (1982, p. 14)

And from Schein:

> the deeper level of *basic assumptions* and *beliefs* that are shared by members of an organization, that operate unconsciously, and that define in a basic "taken-for-granted" fashion an organization's view of itself and its environment. (1985, p. 6)

In these three quotations, only the word "unconsciously" in the last is somewhat problematic, since in many cases employees are well aware of the constraints of the culture. Beyer (1981), for example, distinguishes usefully between ideologies and values as each may independently affect decision making. In fact, as Goodenough (1970, p. 41) notes, participants in a group must know the culture in order to be fully functioning members, who can decode the cultural meanings and shape them into efficient guides to everyday behavior. Schein (1984) indicates further that organizational culture represents the accumulation of assumptions that a group has developed as it has learned both to adapt to changes in outside environments and

---

ture of mind and matter), it tends to obscure the boundaries between the phenomenological character of culture and its more material manifestations, boundaries that serve diagnostically (even if *somewhat* artificially) to discriminate the two phenomena. The interactionist perspective also suggests that culture is more of a dependent variable.

to manage the internal conflicts that inevitably arise. These assumptions are passed on to inductees to the organization, who have been attracted to the organization partially by its culture.

Cultures play enormously important functions in the life and work of organizations. Successful enculturation of an institution, or its "infusion with value" (Selznick, 1957), provides a "substitute for leadership" (cf. Kerr & Jermier, 1978) or an omnipresent, but incorporeal, supervisor surrogate that guides behavior in organizationally desirable ways. As Deal and Kennedy note:

> A strong culture is a system of informal rules that spells out how people are to behave most of the time. By knowing what exactly is expected of them, employees will waste little time in deciding how to act in a given situation. In a weak culture, on the other hand, employees waste a good deal of time just trying to figure out what they should do and how they should do it. The impact of a strong culture on productivity is amazing. In the extreme, we estimate that a company can gain as much as one or two hours of productive work per employee per day. (1982, p. 15)

Cultures in their pristine, disembodied corporate form, however, are rarely if ever identical with the images of each individual in the organization. Indeed, in an organization made up of numerous departmental satrapies as in higher education, there is not likely to be any one culture. Nor are cultures linked causally through what Weick (1979) refers to as "consensually validated grammar." In academia, culture is enacted as myth, as much as map (though, as is explained below, this is not without its positive functions for the organization).

Also to be recognized is the validity of Marxian notions that construe structure as designed and articulated by the dominant organizational coalition. Any managed structure generates a culture supportive of that coalition, thus, allegedly, intimately linking culture, structure, and behavior. In a system characterized by collegiality, however, the assumption is that the coalition that leads the organization is not, after all, exploitive. Each of the other four structures noted in Figure 5.1 — anarchy/polity, bureaucracy, oligarchy, and clan/family — will, on the other hand, reflect the values of the dominant coalitions, in terms of the definitions of culture and structure, the interactions between them, and the ultimate effects on members of the organization.

The definition of culture that is proposed suggests that the concepts of structure and culture can be utilized more constructively as diagnostics if they are first recognized as separate phenomena, leaving until later the discussion the impact of one on the other. Indeed, Meyer and Rowan (1977) are correct in saying that a culture reflects the "myths" of the outside environment in which the institution exists. The more these external contexts are rich in tradition and ritual, the less internal control is exercised through structural means and the more managerial time is devoted to abstract policy framing. Thus, for example, in the context of higher education, where "academic freedom," among other professional-wide traditions, is reified, organizational elites engage heavily in articulation and promulgation of informal agreements that govern faculty behavior with respect to academic freedom, instead of involving themselves substantively in each problematic circumstance.

Collegiality as culture (hereinafter called "c-collegiality"), then, is more than any one organizational culture or "saga"; it is an academic culture, endemic to the profession as a whole (cf. Clark, 1983). It constitutes a "feeder" culture (Louis, 1985), which is initiated through the professionalization processes of graduate school, solidified in the early employment experience, hypostatized in the later career, and, indeed, promulgated as gospel by the mature professional academic. Coming to the "religion" of c-collegiality is a *sine qua non* of life in academia (though "many's the slip 'twixt cup and lip").

In general, invocations of the culture of collegiality are often romantic appeals to the relatively few cases in the history of higher education where it has been prominently employed in the defense of one or another tradition. For most academics, c-collegiality connotes a set of values and beliefs surrounding the idea of participatory democracy, particularly the notion that "stakeholders" have rights to be heard and, in certain circumstances, to have their voices counted (Chell, 1985). The reverse is also true. Collegiality as culture means the willingness to yield some privileges of participation in the belief that peer/professional values respect the rights of the individual. The belief lies in both the general acceptance of the correctness of the value as well as the assumption that it is widely held in the particular college community. That is, faculty not only hold the value themselves, but feel that it is shared sufficiently that transgressions will be seen negatively and will be punished, usually in some subtle form. Thus, as noted above, the twin values — belief in structural rationality and trust in others — are central to c-collegiality.

For some, c-collegiality is seen as the very essence of postsecondary institutional life, where the fundamental social norm of reciprocity is most obviously cherished and practiced. For others, it is assumed to be more of a pervasive psychological emollient, inhabiting the pores of the academic body and sweetening the smell of the sweat of hard-fought, zero-sum political decisions. The truth, as usual, falls in between and is contingent on a number of organizational factors, including size, professionalization of faculty, and degree offerings of the institution.

Interestingly, size of institution does not seem to affect the *definition* of c-collegiality (though, as will be seen below, it does suggest some modifications in the definition of the structures that constitute collegiality). One might expect that small size would make for a *Gemeinschaft*-type community, where norm salience and norm enforcement would be strong. On the other hand, one might also surmise that in a large organization, *Gesellschaft*-type values might prevail, since with more heterogeneity of fields, uniformity of beliefs would be less likely and sanctions more difficult to administer. Yet, this seems not to be the case. The culture of collegiality appears to be similar throughout academia, regardless of type or size of institution. The reason, in part, is that the structure of collegiality (see below) may effectively replace the culture of collegiality in large institutions as a major source of input to individual behavior. To use the Cohen and March (1974) terminology, on smaller campuses, c-collegiality is undergirded with a "consensus metaphor," while on larger campuses, a "democratic metaphor" is more likely to prevail.

In sum, c-collegiality impresses itself on both the organizational structure and the individuals who staff it. In the first instance, again as will be demonstrated below, c-collegiality reinforces the legitimacy of a participatory decision-making structure, even as it obviates the need to use it. C-collegiality constitutes a powerful symbolic presence that serves to mitigate anxieties of incomplete or inadequate opportunities for participation. It thus serves a decidedly political *qua* organizational function by legitimizing the structure of collegiality and the patterns of behavior that follow from it (cf. Rosner, 1983). It also reduces the social awkwardness of status differences brought on by asymmetries of power, which are unacceptable in academic life. As Clark notes with respect to "organizational saga," a concept embracing the culture of collegiality:

> An organizational saga is thus a valuable resource, created over a number of years out of the social components of the formal enterprise. As participants become ideologues, their common definition becomes a foundation for trust and for extreme loyalty. (1972, p. 183)

Further:

> A saga-enriched culture also helps to turn the organization into a community, emotionally warming the institution and giving individuals a sense of place. (1983, p. 83)

Collegiality as Structure

Discussions of the term "collegiality" considered as a structure for decision making also abound in the literature. This meaning will be labeled "s-collegiality" to distinguish it from "c-collegiality." Structure, in the literature of organizational theory, typically is defined as a pattern or design by which organizations are divided and integrated. Sometimes, in addition, it refers to the activities and communications conducted through the structure.[3] It represents the modes by which the organization has aggregated its workers and the means by which the work of the separated groups is coordinated. S-collegiality is concerned primarily with the latter. In still other words, it is associated with the modes of decision making that link units of the organization (individual personnel as well as whole departments) and regulate their activities.[4] The popular academic image of s-collegiality reflects somewhat simplistically a rather ambiguous structure for participation, especially concerning the manner of participation of workers at various levels. It is the purpose of this section to unravel the complexities of that image.

A variety of modes for linking separated units in an organization are possible. Mintzberg's typology, described earlier, offers five modes commonly found in organizations: mutual adjustment, standardization of work processes, standardization of work outputs, standardization of worker skills, and direct supervision (cf. Thompson, 1967; Ouchi & Maguire, 1975). A brief review of the discussion above recalls the means of identifying which of these linking modes are most commonly used in institutions of higher learning.

---

3. The concept of "structure" is defined variously in the literature. See, for example, Mintzberg, 1979; Ranson, Hinings, & Greenwood, 1980; and Wilmott, 1985.

4. Ignored, for the moment, are organizational design questions that involve strategic changes in both the aggregation criteria and the linking mechanisms, both of which may be determined through collegial means. Commonly, such changes are infrequent.

Two of the possibilities are immediately ruled out. Given the great differences in faculty teaching and research techniques and the tradition of academic freedom, "work processes" are hardly ever standardized as a mode of control. Further, since the range of inputs to the institution (both in students and knowledge) varies considerably, work outputs can be expected to diverge, different students and faculty starting at different places and progressing at different rates. Hence, "standardization of outputs" is too difficult to establish and monitor, nor, in many views, is it desirable as a control technique.

Colleges and universities do use the other three modes of coordination in Mintzberg's model. For example, through their recruitment and employment policies, most institutions "standardize worker skills." That is, the faculty at any one institution may be expected to be relatively homogeneous in background, training, and skill levels. Indeed, standardization of worker competencies is the essence of professional preparation.

Institutions of higher learning also use "mutual adjustment" and "direct supervision," and it is through these modes that collegiality is primarily exercised. By "mutual adjustment" Mintzberg means "the coordination of work by the simple process of informal communication." (As noted in Chapter 3, however, the relative isolation of academic research endeavors makes mutual adjustment a relatively infrequent requirement, and the interaction habits carry over to the teaching area, to the detriment of that process.) Direct supervision, on the other hand, is the process of issuing instructions to and the monitoring of work of one person by another. Supervision is managed through a formal system of authority distributed in some fashion among the participants of an organization, the particular domains of authority dictated (formally, at least) by the competencies of the participants. In a Weberian bureaucracy, the competencies are arranged in a formal hierarchy of authority established by promotion or recruitment of the most demonstrably able, while in a college or university, authority of different types (e.g., the authority of expertise, the authority of bureaucracy) is variously distributed, often ambiguously.

In sum, given standardization of professional preparation (homogeneous faculty input for any given institution), the organizational structure of a college or university can be identified through the authority structure for supervision (really "indirect supervision") and through the processes of mutual adjustment. S-collegiality is concerned with the first of these; b-collegiality, discussed below, is at the heart of the second. Institutions that are deemed to have collegial structures (s-collegiality) are typically believed to conform to a recognizable pattern of authority to regulate the activities of their members. As noted earlier, the particular form of collegiality is a function at least in part of the culture and goals of the organization (which themselves are partly determined by the dominant power coalition). The joining of the "maps" of Helsabeck and Kilmann points to different configurations that vary in the degree and nature of their collegiality. Collegial structures will be found more frequently to use "mutual adjustment" in contrast to direct supervision as a mode of coordination. They will also more frequently decouple the administrative and academic sides of decision making, decentralizing to the faculty decisions that in other circumstances would suggest greater administrative oversight.

It might be argued, of course, that decentralization is the result of a wresting away of power and authority by the faculty from the administration on the grounds that the latter are neither competent to participate in faculty matters nor trustworthy enough to share faculty secrets. It is important to distinguish, therefore, similar appearing decision-making structures in colleges and universities. While they may look alike, what distinguishes those that are "collegial" are the norms of c-collegiality. Participatory structures without c-collegiality are not "collegial" in the common sense of the term, but are merely political.

It could also be argued that a collegial institution might exist without s-collegiality provided c-collegiality were strong enough. That is, it is possible to conceive of an institution so heavily embued with c-collegiality (i.e., high in trust and rationality) that an outsider would see the institution as collegial, even in the absence of formal mechanisms to preserve collegiality. While such an institution, necessarily small, might exist for short periods, it would be essentially unstable, relying on saga usually created through the charisma of one individual.

In the model presented in Chapter 1, a number of variables were hypothesized to influence the shape of the organizational structure. In other chapters, the nature of information requirements, the need for coordination, and the exercise of power were discussed. Here, the concern is with the influence of c-collegiality on the shape and character of the decision-making structure. The modes of discussion and descriptions of structure that were employed earlier (the models of Helsabeck and Kilmann) will be helpful here, but it is necessary first to consider more carefully the critical concept of "authority."

As Katz and Kahn (1978, p. 324) noted, authority has to do with the "pattern and scope of influence transactions in the organization." Pattern and scope, of course, can be identified by an analysis of organizational structure, while influence transactions may be understood in terms of interactions found to be "caused" by the exercise of power. Specifically, the exercise of organizational authority can be observed when legitimacy is accorded to the potential use of certain positive and negative sanctions by individuals or collections of individuals — that is, when it is recognized by the organizational participants that the organization has formally deeded a unit (a person or decision-making body) the "right" and "power" to enforce a decision. Thus, a person may understand not only that he/she is subject to another person's or body's influence, but that he/she may, indeed, be a member of a body with that right and power.

While structure is manifested in the division of labor and role specification, authority is both manifest and phenomenological. The collective expectations of organizational participants with respect to the formal sanctions available to certain roles within the structure act (invisibly) to constrain behavior, while the behavior itself is observable.

In colleges and universities, structure, then, is the agreed-upon distribution of sets of activities and interactions in which faculty and administrators engage as they link units of the organization, and it is as well the equally accepted rules (and sanctions for broken rules) for adjudicating disputes and evaluating personnel. To understand how collegiality is embodied in the structure of *some*, but not all, colleges and universities, a meaningful way of describing the distribution of supervisory roles and the rules of adjudication and sanctioning must be found. That is, it is important to see whether there are some distinctive structures that somehow lend themselves to the incorporation of the dimensions of collegiality noted earlier — namely, rationality and trust.

There are a number of typologies of organizations or organizational structures in the extant literature, each defined by variables deemed critical by their creators. Perrow (1970; cf. Woodward, 1965), for example, uses "technology" (defined in terms of number of exceptions to raw material and analyzability of procedures for transformation) to yield four categories of organization — craft, nonroutine, routine, and engineering. Pfeffer (1977) describes institutions in terms of the degree to which their participants agree on goals and on the means to achieve them, yielding, again, four types — political, bureaucratic, collegial, and anarchic (cf. Becher, 1984). Blau (1973) uses bureaucratic criteria to classify organizations. The Aston group and its successors have developed a variety of indices of organizational structure. But none of these approaches quite accurately or comprehensively enough captures the nuances of collegiality. What is needed is a schema that distinguishes institutions that are structured in a highly collegial way from those that are not.

Beyer and Lodahl (1976) move closer to filling this need by utilizing the concepts of "decentralization" and "collegiality" in a description of structure, noting that they are not identical. The first refers to the extent to which an institution is "divided into subunits that exercise substantial control over a range of decisions relevant to their own functioning," while the second means the degree of opportunity by faculty "to exercise influence, either by direct vote, or through mechanisms of representation on senates or committees, in decisions relevant to such central work tasks as teaching and research." Essentially, this approach considers both substantive decision making and political equity in describing the structure of a university. Another approach (Helsabeck, 1973) considers quite similar dimensions but uses them diagnostically to create potential maps of authority structures. This latter system, described in some depth earlier, will be recapitulated here.

Colleges and universities, according to Helsabeck, can be placed in a framework for classification that measures their strength on two independent dimensions: (1) the location in the organization where decisions are made (e.g., from highly centralized to highly decentralized), and (2) the degree of participation (e.g., from complete involvement of all persons to absolute power of one person). Thus, one can imagine decision making taking place in the community as a whole, with either mass participation or no participation (e.g., via autocratic decisions). On the other hand, one can conceive of the same decision making being decentralized, again with either mass or no participation. Further, the particularly important substantive domains in which organizational decisions in colleges and universities fall — authority allocation, resource allocation, resource acquisition, and production — can be seen to be dispersed in an infinite variety of ways throughout the structure for dealing with them (i.e., locating each of the four decision domains in one of the four quadrants formed by the axes of centralization — "centricity" in Helsabeck's terms — and degree of participation).

To illustrate briefly, a variation in degree of participation can be seen in the framework for decisions about how to dispense discretionary funds available at the departmental level. At one institution, decisions might be made in a monocratic way (by the chair), while at another, mass democracy (the entire departmental faculty) might be the mode. Similarly, variations across institutions can be noted in the degree of "centricity." For example, decisions about admissions (a resource acquisition-type decision) at one college might be made centrally; at a different institution, the activity might be decentralized to the individual department. Figure 5.2 casts these alternatives in a graphic format.

Returning to the definition of authority above, it is conceived of as the organizational legitimation of these rights of jurisdiction and participation. By this definition, s-collegiality can be manifested in only two of the four quadrants in Figure 5.2, namely, "disaggregated" and "clan." That is, for s-collegiality to exist, participation must be possible in some form. The titular structure most typically erected to permit collegial decision making is either consensual or representative democracy, including faculty in its membership (and frequently administrative staff and students). Academic and/or institutional "senates" are common. The assumption in collegial institutions is that these arenas for decision making keep open the rights of participation and hence influence, so that in cases of violation or alleged violation of organizational members' interests, there

Figure 5.2
Alternative Decision-Making Structures

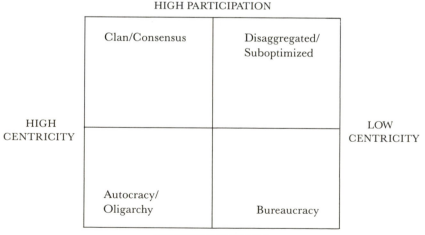

HIGH PARTICIPATION

Clan/Consensus	Disaggregated/ Suboptimized
Autocracy/ Oligarchy	Bureaucracy

HIGH CENTRICITY — LOW CENTRICITY

LOW PARTICIPATION

Partly adapted from Helsabeck (1973, p. 6).

exists a standing structure for redress. That is, the structure may or may not be used, depending in part on alternative and informal structures that act as well in their stead. When pressed, most members of collegial organizations will admit that many "real" decisions do not take place in the setting of the formal structures, but elsewhere in the institution.

Nevertheless, the *formal* apparatus of participative decision making in the context of collegial culture as defined above is usually required to demonstrate to the organizational participants that the institution is "rational" and "trustworthy." In Gamson's (1968) terms, participants in the organization will have high confidence in the system's capacity and the authority's willingness to act in their behalf. "Confidence in the political institutions means that the group believes either that these institutions produce authorities who are its agents or else produce favorable decisions regardless of the particular incumbents" (Gamson, 1968, p. 54). The system and/or its members are trustworthy.

The converse is also true. The mere presence of participatory rights does not alone ensure collegiality. To reiterate, the rights of participation and even the apparatus of participation are necessary but not sufficient conditions for s-collegiality. They must be present for collegiality to exist, but they do not alone guarantee collegiality. As noted above, colleges or universities may incorporate representative, participative structures, but if trust and rationality are lacking, there will not be s-collegiality (and the institution will not be known as collegial).

Hence, what defines s-collegiality is some (but not any one particular) arrangement of participatory rights and memberships that incorporates the beliefs and values of c-collegiality. S-collegiality is the *organization's* manifestation of c-collegiality, just as b-collegiality (behavior collegiality — see below) is, on the idiographic level, the *individual's* manifestation of c-collegiality. S-collegiality both symbolizes collegiality and gives visible evidence that it can be maintained in adversity. It is the mode of interpenetration of the culture and social system through the process of "institutionalization," to use the functionalist paradigm of Talcott Parsons. Finally, s-collegiality is also the "subjective meaning" that organization members attach to a decision-making structure (Smircich, 1983; cf. Goodenough, 1970). In the language of Argyris and Schon (1974), s-collegiality permits a merging of theories-in-use and theories-in-practice such that the ideology of democratic or participative decision making is perceived to be present in the visible structure for decision making.

Collegiality as Behavior

The third conceptualization of collegiality can now be considered. Just as it was suggested above that c-collegiality was a nexus of beliefs and values embedded in the professional and corporate culture of an institution and that s-collegiality was a framework for expression of those beliefs and values, here it is argued that collegiality should also be understood as behaviors reflecting both. Called "b-collegiality," it stands to mean in essence the complex of actions taken by faculty and administrators in playing out their various institutional roles as they are "shaped" by c-collegiality and s-collegiality.

When role behavior in higher education is discussed, it refers to both line and staff functions performed by faculty and administrators.[5] The behavior encompasses two categories of behavior separated by time: (1) decisions about what should be done (either by self or other[s]), and (2) the execution of those decisions (by self). Further, behavior is taken either individually or in groups. Thus, role enactment covers the range of behaviors of faculty and administrators as they act out their various roles in staff or policy-making and/or in line activities. For example (and somewhat less abstractly), a typical faculty role might include teaching, research, and work on the academic senate or its committees. The faculty role thus refers not only to individual and collective decision making, but also to the patterns of relationships and interactions among colleagues as they perform their line/task functions.

In characterizing this third element of collegiality — b-collegiality — it is important to differentiate role behavior, which is a normally expected playing out of the faculty role, from behavior that not only corresponds to the institutional role expectation, but reflects, *in addition*, the influence of c- and s-collegiality. As Homans (1950) notes, there is a set of behaviors, interactions, and sentiments that is "required," and there is another set that "emerges" as a result of a variety of organizational conditions (e.g., the impossibility of complete specification of duties, and the norms and values in the institution). What characterizes b-collegiality, then, is not simply the enactment of the various roles called for in any (or, perhaps most) institutions of higher education, but the modification of those roles to account for c- and s-collegiality.

More empirical research is needed to separate "normal" behavior

---

5. For this discussion, however, references are primarily to faculty members.

from collegial role behavior.[6] A start has been made by Finkelstein (1981), for example, in a study in which faculty were asked to describe the nature of their professional relationships with individuals either within or outside of their institutions. The author identified what he labeled "dimensions of collegueship," such as "critical feedback on professional writing," "help in identifying sources of research support," and "general intellectual stimulation." The question is, however, whether these behaviors are specifically "collegial" or are simply the "expected" role behavior of faculty in institutions of higher learning.

In classic role theory terms (cf. Katz & Kahn, 1978), role behavior results from an actor's interpretation of the sent role as it is mediated by personality and institutional conditions, such as system norms and values. Role definition in higher education, however, is exemplary in its looseness (more so in institutions that are more complex and differentiated). Indeed, the sparseness in professional and institutional specification of modes for carrying out the roles, as well as the relative weights the institution places on various activities constituting the roles, is a source both of faculty satisfaction (via their autonomy and academic freedom) and of frustration (through misplaced energies in search of institutional rewards).

This is not say that the "system" is anarchic, as Cohen and March (1974) suggest. Rather, it indicates only that the *transformational* roles of faculty are relatively more open. On the other hand, the system maintenance roles, covering the nontransformational roles of faculty (e.g., in regulating inputs, outputs, and feedback), in which faculty engage are clearly more specified. Hence, as pointed out in the Introduction, there is little reason to assert that anarchy is rampant in higher education. But it is largely with the nontransformational roles that s-collegiality is concerned. To be somewhat more precise, while the exact nature of faculty roles within governance committees is not clearly specified, the roles of the committees in the overall governance structure are quite well known and understood by members of the institution.

If individual roles, then, are broadly delineated, role expectations must be understood as a combination of very general formal institutional requirements and an informal and still fairly loose specification emerging out of system-wide and local norms (cf. Becher & Kogan, 1980). The latter may vary dramatically from those ceremo-

---

6. For an exhaustive list of faculty activities and roles, see Bess, 1982.

nialized universalistically by the professionalization myths of gradu-ate school to institutionally idiosyncratic ones. In point of fact, there exist at least six sources of the role requirements, which impress themselves in varying degrees on every faculty member:

1. An idealized faculty role transmitted by the profession — es-sentially, collegiality espoused and/or myths and wishes about the role.
2. A generalized faculty role transmitted by the academic com-munity sector in which the institution stands (e.g., in the Carnegie classification) and accepted as reasonable for the type of institution.
3. The formal role expectations transmitted by the local institu-tion.
4. The informal role expectations transmitted by the local cam-pus culture.
5. The formal and informal role expectations transmitted by the discipline or department at the local institution.
6. The role expectations of the faculty member transmitted by him/herself.

These relationships can perhaps best be sorted out by depicting the differences in graphic form. In Figure 5.3, the six modes of understanding the faculty role and their separate and integrated impacts on behavior are shown. Between these sets of expectations, there arise several "zones of ambiguity," the solutions to which yield the varying approaches to collegiality found at different institutions of higher education.[7]

Having identified the various role possibilities, it is necessary now to consider what is meant by "behavior collegiality" (b-collegial-ity). It is submitted here that b-collegiality exists under conditions of role clarity and congruence of two types. First, collective decision making as a faculty role will embody b-collegiality when institution-al type faculty roles and campus mandated roles (I and C) approach the image of collegiality as idealized in the profession (P) — that is, when $P = I, C$. For example, if faculty roles identified for state col-leges are coincident with (or at least do not do serious violence to) ideal collegial values, and if a particular state college espouses those

---

7. In effect, these are variations of what March and Olsen (1976, p. 12) call the "ambiguity of organization," one of four types of ambiguity facing decision makers.

Figure 5.3
Role Conceptions, Role Behavior, and
Zones of Ambiguity

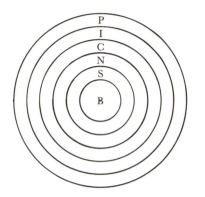

Role Conceptualizations*

P = Idealized Professional Role
    (collegiality espoused)
I = Institutional Type Faculty Role
    (from Carnegie classification)
C = Campus Mandated Faculty Role
    (by institutional type — Ex. 1)
N = Emergent Informal Role Norms
    (combining role sources 4 and
    5 from text)
S = Self-sent Role
B = Role Behavior

Zones of Personal Ambiguity

P – I   Ambiguity of Professionalization/Socialization
I – C   Ambiguity of Institutional Differentiation
C – B   Ambiguity of Local Sanctions
P – S   Ambiguity of Guilt
P – C   Ambiguity of Collegiality
I – B   Ambiguity of Education and Training
S – B   Ambiguity of Skill

*Representing sent roles by mapping role senders in concentric circles is a traditional mode of understanding the pressures on organizational members. What is added here is the set of phenomenological pressures experienced by faculty members.

values, then b-collegiality will be more likely to exist. Second, collegial behavior as a faculty role will take place when the self-sent role (S) of a majority of the faculty is congruent with the idealized professional role (P) — that is, S = P. In other words, if the idealized collegial role has been sufficiently institutionalized, or, in Selznick's (1957) words, when there has been a widespread "institutionalization of value," collegiality will become a reality. Emergent norms (N) will then support and constrain role behavior that approximates the ideal (P) — that is, N = P.

For each of the five types of institutions in Figure 5.1 — collegium, clan/family, oligarchy, bureaucracy, and anarchy/polity —

there exists a different combination of role expectations of the types noted above. What being a faculty member means differs in each institution, in terms of what is expected and what duties are performed. That is, first, the "required" activities (I and C) are different; second, the embellishments that are *expected* to "emerge" to flesh out the role (N) differ; and third, the role with its embellishments is played differently at different institutions (B).

In the explanatory terms provided by Argyris and Schon (1974), the "espoused role" on various campuses differs by institutional type and, since role expectations have at least six sources (as above), is often not held uniformly. Moreover, the behavior in use will also diverge. More specifically, what will be seen in four of the five institutional types identified in Figure 5.1 are role behaviors that depart from the presumed norm of collegiality to the extent that the institutions incorporate either trust or rationality or both. In the fifth, the collegium, where theories espoused and in use are isomorphic, there will be no variation from the ideal behavior. However, in all five cases, there will be ambiguities about the nature of the role.[8]

Given the large number of behaviors in the faculty repertory, a concrete description of the nature of the modifications of roles that characterize collegial behavior is beyond the scope of this chapter. It is possible, however, to use the key dimensions of c-collegiality to predict very generally the character of interactions among faculty and administrators in collegial institutions. For example, if trust and rationality help determine c-collegiality, it might be reasonable to expect to see behavior in a collegial institution reflecting these values (Zand, 1972). As noted above, trust refers largely to expectations of organizational participants with respect to other participants (interpersonal relations), while rationality has to do with the participants' expectations about the institution's intentions and reliability. Thus, there would likely be much sharing of information, tolerance of opinions different from one's own, and assistance in professional and personal matters.

Above it was suggested that b-collegiality conceivably exists in any of the five institutional types, depending on the degree to which trust and rationality are present in c- and s-collegiality. As indicated

---

8. Research is needed on the relative strengths of c-collegiality and s-collegiality as together they may have an impact on role behavior. What, for example, is the effect of a weak c-collegiality in combination with a strong s-collegiality, or the reverse?

in Figure 5.1, however, the likelihood is different for different types. Hypothetically, the following represents the proximity of role behavior at each type of institution to b-collegiality:

Anarchy/Polity — Random compliance, as anomic conditions make it uncertain what the expectation is. All of the ambiguities are maximized.

Bureaucracy — Little compliance. The ambiguity and/or weakness of P and N are replaced by distrust, removing the force of the norm of reciprocity.

Oligarchy — Compliance by faculty who value the favor of the coalition in power and who believe that the rationality of the decision-making system will ultimately reward them.

Clan/Family — Uneven compliance, as some faculty are uncertain whether the structure and leadership will be supportive of this behavior.

Collegium — Much compliance, since faculty strongly believe that the behavior will be reciprocated and that the system will reward or at least not penalize this kind of assistance.

This is not to say, of course, that behavior invariably corresponds either to the professional ideal or to the local norm — for any of the five institutional types. Faculty, as all human beings, are imperfect in the execution of their tasks. Hence, departures from ideal or local expectations may be expected because of human fallibility, as well as external or internal pressures. Interestingly, it is through the modes of addressing this very human condition that institutions of higher learning most clearly express b-collegiality. That is, the ways in which faculty "cover" for colleagues' shortcomings tells much about the presence or absence of b-collegiality.

This can be illustrated through one typical faculty role — teaching undergraduates. In the idealized, espoused role common to all five types of institutions, the role expectation is that faculty dedicate themselves to maximizing student growth and achievement (however that may be defined on an individual campus). Imagine a situation in which a faculty member is not able to perform because of a temporary illness and seeks a colleague's assistance as a temporary stand-in. Such a request in a collegial institution, one would predict, would be honored not only without hesitation, but with commitment, while in a noncollegial institution, either the class would not be covered or would be superficially so.

One further distinction between collegial and noncollegial institutions must be noted. That is the modes by which behavior in violation of norms is sanctioned. These will differ according to the levels of trust and rationality that exist. Referring again to Figure 5.1, it can be predicted that where trust is high, both positive and negative sanctions will be applied. However, in clan-like institutions, enforcement of collegiality will be idiosyncratic and probably inconsistent, as charismatic leadership asserts its influence. Where trust is low, with low rationality (e.g., more anarchic conditions), weak and few sanctions will exist, since all norms will be weak in an anarchy (save, perhaps, those forwarded by the dominant coalition, which are minimally needed to preserve the anarchy). And where trust is low and rationality is high, violations of role behavior will be sanctioned formally, since the structure of the system itself, rather than its values, is perceived as legitimate.

What has been discussed thus far with respect to b-collegiality is largely concerned with the nature of interpersonal relations among colleagues as they perform their "transformational" functions — teaching, research, and service. As noted above, b-collegiality may also be present in the context of collective decision making. When c-collegiality is present in an institution, role behavior tends to be more task focussed, since there is trust and stability in interpersonal relations. Hence, collective decision making in an s-collegiality format is directed toward solving real organizational problems. On the other hand, when c-collegiality is absent, collective decision making will be occupied much more with issues of equity and personal benefits — protecting the individual against the presumed malevolence of either formal organizational authorities or the dominant coalition. The behavior of faculty in an s-collegiality setting tends to be open and informal. In a setting where collegiality is not present, role behavior will tend to be stylized, formal, and constrained by rules.

Functions of Collegiality

Collegiality has both immediate and instrumental functions in colleges and universities, and it serves both individual and organizational needs. The familiar Parsons (1951) functionalist paradigm discussed in Chapter 1 illustrates the roles that collegiality plays. In Figure 5.4, the four functional needs of all social systems are displayed, with the services provided by collegiality inserted in the cells.

Figure 5.4
Functions of Collegiality

	INSTRUMENTAL	CONSUMMATORY
INTERNAL	(Latency) 1. C-collegiality provides means of socialization, norm establishment, standard setting, and behavior control 2. S-collegiality gives stability and confidence in existing grievance recourse; opportunity for social interaction across subunit boundaries; satisfactions from participation	(Integration) 3. C-collegiality provides incentive to maximize satisfactions of inter-unit and interpersonal interaction 4. S-collegiality offers forum for conflict indentification and resolution
EXTERNAL	(Adaptation) 5. C-collegiality provides sense of equity in distribution of resources 6. S-collegiality gives opportunity for efficient acquisition and internal distribution of resources, given decentralization	(Goal Attainment) 7. C-collegiality offers institutional continuity of image and purpose, permitting efficient recruitment of students and faculty and placement of graduates 8. S-collegiality permits identification of and commitment of departments to specific environmental domains of concern; restricts overlap and permits satisfactions with achievements both of subunit and institution.

It could be argued, of course, that other cultural values and other structural forms might be substituted for c-collegiality and s-collegiality, with the same functions still served. This is true. The functionalist paradigm recognizes on a general level the prerequisite needs of a social system. Indeed, as has been shown, several different kinds of institutions of higher learning seem to exist, with varying degrees of collegiality embodied in them. The question might be raised as to whether configurations other than collegial ones are "efficient" in higher education—efficient in the sense that they attend well both to the needs of the institution and to the needs of the participants. As has been asserted throughout this book, it is important to refer to various "contingencies" to answer the question. For example, Wilkins and Ouchi (1983) suggest that the efficiency of an organizational design depends on the nature of the environment external to the organization (cf. Weick, 1984) and the "fit" between the organization and the environment (Van de Ven & Drazin, 1985). Wilkins and Ouchi indicate, for example, that clan-type control mechanisms may not be as efficient as other forms when complexity and uncertainty are relatively low or moderate. As they note:

> The clan may require the development and maintenance of too much social agreement to be efficient under less ambiguous transactional conditions. On the other hand, the clan will be more efficient . . . under conditions of ambiguity, complexity, and interdependence of transactions. (1983, p. 477)

The other forms of organization noted in Figure 5.1 also are more or less efficient depending on environmental and other contingencies— for example, technology and environment, as noted earlier. Under highly stable and predictable external conditions, as one instance, bureaucracies tend to be highly efficient.

It is necessary here to return to the theme of Chapter 1 and the integration of the thinking of Helsabeck and Kilmann to describe the various stuctures of decision making that are possible. For various kinds of organizational concerns, decisions can be dispersed in various ways and can be described in terms of their location on two axes—centricity of control and degree of participation (Helsabeck, 1973). Kilmann (1977) suggests a variety of structural patterns, each of which, in the schema presented here, might "fit" in any of the four Helsabeck quadrants. However, Kilmann notes that each of the configurations is likely to be more effective than the others in addressing certain problems or "prerequisites." As organizations typically move through cycles of problems, it is likely that collegial forms will be found to be more or less efficient, depending on the predominant prerequisite at the time (see Chapter 8).

The virtually ubiquitous press toward short-run efficiency as a desideratum in American society is no less present in colleges and universities, particularly in days of budget depression. There arises, therefore, the question of whether collegial structures should be sacrificed in the name of short-term efficiency. One answer, perhaps, lies in understanding the unique nature of the academic profession. Professional preparation of academics predisposes them to have a relatively homogeneous set of expectations of one another regardless of the requirements of efficiency. Hence, s-collegiality may be a requisite structure to maintain the "rationality" (as defined in this chapter) of faculty, even if it may not be the most efficient mechanism for dealing with organizational matters. Further, there is some reason to believe that collegial structures may, indeed, be more functional for universities in "good" times. Assuming that on average there are more good than bad times, and given the considerable period required to institutionalize collegial values on a college campus, it may be wiser to suffer the penalties of short-term inefficiencies in the interests of preserving the structure and supportive values needed for efficiency in the long run.

In sum, this chapter has addressed the need for a more precise explication of the nature of "collegiality" in higher education. The concept has been employed in many ways, perhaps most commonly as the panacea for most institutional ills. What has been attempted here is to separate the three essential components of collegiality — the culture of collegiality, the structure of collegiality, and the behavior of collegiality — in order better to understand each alone and to comprehend how they are integrated. In addition, the chapter constituted an effort to demythologize the concept by articulating the various functions served by collegiality. It was noted that the concepts of "trust" and "belief in rationality" seem essential to an understanding of collegiality and that it is possible to conceive of institutions that embody certain structures as more or less likely to be collegial, depending on the extent to which these concepts inhere in the institutions.

As Dill notes:

One difficulty with academic symbols and their supporting rituals is that they are often abstract. They do not immediately communicate with the everyday behaviors of academic life. (1982, p. 315)

In this chapter, the concept of collegiality may have been rendered a bit less mysterious and hence more useful in the management of colleges and universities.

Chapters 2 through 5 have revealed various sources of influence on university decision-making structures. They demonstrated, it is hoped, that decision making in universities is more "determined" than certain currently salient views (e.g., loose coupling or organized anarchy) would suggest. The resolution of the competing influences on any one campus may have the appearance of uniqueness to its participants, but in point of fact there is a pattern to the handful of structures that have evolved. That pattern is described in the next chapter.

CHAPTER

SIX *The Dispersion of Authority*

The chapters just concluded contained a consideration of the variety of ways in which the decision-making structures in colleges and universities may be influenced by vertical and horizontal information flow, by power, and by collegiality. In this chapter, the notions adumbrated earlier will be brought together to suggest more concretely the shape and character of formal decision-making structures in institutions of higher education. The argument that follows moves from the general to the specific. First, an exhaustive array of possible "settings" for decision making is developed. Then, those most frequently found to be formalized as structures in colleges and universities are identified. Next, the settings that are more likely to be found for particular kinds of academic and nonacademic decisions are discussed. Finally, the dispersion of these settings to various parts of the organization as a structure for decisions is laid out and explained.

Types of Settings

Twenty-one kinds of settings seem to constitute an exhaustive list of the decision-making arenas that might be found in higher education. By "settings" is meant simply domains of human activity (intra- or interpersonal) that result in decisions having organizational implications. The settings vary in three important ways: (1) in numbers of persons involved; (2) in employee classification or constituency (e.g., administration or faculty); and (3) in formal vs. informal nature. Thus, for example, a dyadic setting may include two administrators considering a land purchase decision, while a committee might include more than two people and comprise faculty and/or administrators. (For purposes of discussion in this chapter, the informal condition cited in the third category is omitted.)

Students (and others such as parents or community officials; cf. Glenny, 1972) are not included in this analysis since they are clients, rather than members, of the organization. Despite students' physical presence on the campus for extended periods of time and despite their periodic "demand" for an active voice in decision making (e.g., in the late 1960s), their treatment as "clients" or "customers" would appear better to fit their actual status, as perceived and treated by the members of the college or university. However, as the organizational behavior literature is unclear on membership criteria, and as the educational literature on governance frequently includes discussions of students as participants, it is important to justify through some extended treatment their omission here.

One reason for conceptually excluding students from membership is that organizations like colleges and universities are not "polities." Though they clearly have political overtones, and, as has been noted, politics do enter into the decision-making process, they are not subject to the same processual dynamics that polities are (see, for example, the seminal works of Clark, 1967, and Dahl, 1957). For one thing, regardless of Pfeffer type, on an organizational level there is (or, more properly, there is presumed to be) a more commonly shared set of institutional goals, a latent one of which is institutional prestige, that constrains the number of activities that are zero-sum in nature. That is, there appears to be more "integrative" than "distributive" conflict resolution (Thomas, 1976) in organizations as contrasted with communities. More simply, people in organizations, especially those organizations with relatively few nominal goals, are more willing to share than people in a community, where goals are diverse, subtle, and poorly communicated.

Second, while customers or clients of organizations exert a profound influence on the nature of the organization, that influence can be viewed as an environmental contingency with which members of the organization must deal. Member interactions with clients, moreover, are quite different from those with fellow organization members. Employees of organizations are related to one another through a network of more or less interdependent positions representing differentiated parts of the organization. Although there are different types of organizational interdependencies, the requirements for cooperation to accomplish acknowledged institutional objectives demand a degree of comity not required in nonorganizational settings.

Finally, at the individual level, members of organizations are forced to continue to deal with one another on a regular, interpersonal basis after decisions are made, thus requiring a civility and consideration which may not always be found in polities (Blau, 1964; cf. the previous discussion of collegiality in Chapter 5). For these varied reasons, students have been excluded from consideration here as organizational decision makers, and the decision settings noted pertain to administrators and faculty.[1]

To return to the discussion of the decision-making settings, note in Figure 6.1 the array of the 21 possibilities.[2] The 21 settings in this matrix exceed the number typically found in the profit-making sector. The greater number needed to describe the college and university decision-making structure reveals once again the complications brought on by the dual but interacting lines of formal authority of administration and faculty (cf. Lunsford, 1963). In profit-making enterprises, the structure can be more simply portrayed by relabeling the "Faculty" column "production workers" or "line operators" and excising many of the settings in which interaction is not likely to take place. The nature of a hierarchy, that is, makes direct communication between top management and line workers both unlikely and dysfunctional.[3] In higher education, on the other hand, faculty occupy both line and management positions, so that the lines of authority are more complex. Further, as several authors (Stein & Kanter, 1980; Zand, 1981; Bendor, 1985) note, there is a parallel organization that almost invariably exists to augment the formal structure. In academia, parallel structures of both formal and informal character have *de jure* and/or *de facto* authority, depending on the particular decision to be made.

To reiterate the theses here, the nature and strength of the au-

---

1. Having said this, however, it is necessary to make clear that in some respects universities *are* like communities, primarily because of their "loose coupling," but far less so than is commonly believed.

2. There is a similarity between this matrix and that of Mortimer and McConnell (1978, pp. 14–15). These authors suggest that the distribution of authority to various decision makers may be accounted for in terms of the nature of the issue being considered. The analysis here expands the number of explanatory variables and settings.

3. Exceptions to this observation can, of course, be found, but they are not common.

Figure 6.1
Decision-Making Settings
in Higher Education

DECENTRALIZED ⟷ CENTRALIZED

		CONSTITUENT GROUPS		
*FORMATS**		Faculty	Middle Management	Top Management (Admin.)
Assembly *Setting*	Faculty	1	X	X
	Middle Mgmt	2	3	X
	Top Mgmt	4	5	6
Committee *Setting*	Faculty	7	X	X
	Middle Mgmt	8	9	X
	Top Mgmt	10	11	12
Dyadic *Setting*	Faculty	13	X	X
	Middle Mgmt	14	15	X
	Top Mgmt	16	17	18
Single *Person* *Setting*	Faculty	19	X	X
	Middle Mgmt	X	20	X
	Top Mgmt	X	X	21

MASS DEMOCRATIC ↕ MONARCHIC

*Formats correspond roughly to Helsabeck's axis of participation, running from "mass democratic" at the top to "monarchic" at the bottom. (See Figure 2.1, which also reveals the second of Helsabeck's dimensions — centricity — though not quite as definitively.)

thority that these "settings" carry and their dispersion in a structure for decision making are contingent on the following:

1. The decision domain or subdomain (see Chapter 1; cf. Mortimer & McConnell, 1978).
2. The degree and nature of the vertical information requirements (Galbraith, 1977).
3. The needs for organizational coordination laterally (Van de Ven, Delbecq, & Koenig, 1976).

4. The influence of collegiality (see Chapter 5) and politics (Chapter 4; cf. Pfeffer, 1977).

The influences displayed in Figure 6.2 reveal the set of decision realms (the subcategories of inputs, transformations, outputs, and feedback) against the 13 factors that might be thought to have influenced the allocation of authority to one of the 21 decision-making structural types. These factors consist of: A—Galbraith's information contingencies; B—Van de Ven, Delbecq, and Koenig's coordination constraints (both represent the rational constraints that stem from the need for information for efficient decision making); C—the Pfeffer (1977) and Hickson et al. (1971) influences, which represent the political and potentially nonrational forces of influence; D—the impact of collegiality.

The cells of the matrix thus formed may be filled in with the 21 "decision settings" from Figure 6.1. Not all of the cells are filled in, since the purpose here is to suggest a model for understanding the decision-making structure in higher education, not to lay out an exhaustive set of testable propositions. To be inserted in the matrix, then, are the various settings where the types of decisions can take place. For each realm of decision (more correctly, for each "sub-realm" of decision) there are 21 possible decision settings. The constraints or contingencies (A through D) describe the influences that help predict the particular setting. There may be, indeed usually are, competing influences among the 13. Hence, for some decisions, the prediction from the contingencies may call for different settings among the 21 possibilities, reflecting the ambiguity of power and influence over certain domains. What will be found, in fact, is that the closer an institution comes to being "collegial," the more consistent will be the prediction of the settings—that is, the less often different settings will appear in a vertical column for a particular decision. The converse is also true. The more an institution is non-rational or political, the more frequently different settings will appear in a column. In still other words, as colleges and universities become more rational, participants come to see the institution as such. They come to believe in the mechanisms for decision making and to trust one another. The loci for decision making—that is, the settings and their placement throughout the organization—become known and predictable.

In the next section, a very brief illustration of these various influences in one domain—inputs (undergraduate admissions)—is presented.

Figure 6.2
The Allocation of Decisions to Decision Settings

REALMS OF DECISIONS

CONSTRAINTS/ CONTINGENCIES*	Inputs			Transformations			Outputs		Feedback
	Undergraduate Admissions	*Faculty Recruitment and Evaluation*	*Tuition and External Support*	*Teaching*	*Research*	*Service*	*Graduates of the Institution*	*Knowledge Exported from the Institution*	
A1									
A2	10†								
A3									
A4									
A5									
B6	11–14								
B7	20–21								
B8	10–13								

C9   10
C10
C11   1, 2, 4, 5, 7
D12   16, 17
D13   17, 18

*Constraints/Contingencies Code

A. Galbraith (1977) – information overload leads to:
1. Environmental management
2. Creation of slack resources
3. Creation of self-contained units
4. More vertical resources
5. More lateral relations

B. Van de Ven, Delbecq, & Koenig (1976) – group vs. bureaucratic coordination:
6. Task uncertainty leads to group coordination
7. Interdependence leads to group coordination
8. Size leads to bureaucratic coordination

C. Pfeffer (1977); Hickson et al. (1971) – power derives from:
9. Uncertainty
10. Unsubstitutability
11. Centrality

D. Bess – collegiality leads to:
12. Rationality
13. Trust

†Numbers in the cells refer to the decision-making settings in the matrix in Figure 6.1. Thus, for example, an A2 constraint is hypothesized to call for an admissions decision in a number 10 setting.

Undergraduate Admissions Decisions

Undergraduate admissions processes vary across institutions, but the objectives of screening and sifting students are common. The intent is to secure a class of students whose aggregate characteristics permit the institution to engage in raw material transformations that satisfy the students and the various constituencies that support them. Too high or too low a level of quality, or too diverse or homogeneous a set of backgrounds, or too rich or too poor, or too conservative or too liberal will prevent the institution from using its personnel and physical resources to transform the students into the "finished" or semi-finished products that the institution manifestly intends. Faculty, for example, cannot teach well in environments for which their own skills and attitudes are not suitable. Universities without proper libraries or physical facilities or social and recreational settings cannot provide the opportunities for intellectual and emotional growth desirable for students. On the other hand, institutions with too great an endowment of these resources will waste them on a student body that, for example, may be poorly equipped intellectually or athletically. (It should be noted, of course, that such "matching" often largely suits faculty interests. Poor "quality" students can best be taught by the most gifted faculty if the latter are disposed to give their attention to the former.)

While the above may be reasonably accurate as a normative (read "rational") description, in point of fact the ideal admissions process is compromised by the diversity of interests within a college or university that seeks to forward its own aims with respect to admissions. As above, various forces (information needs, power, and collegiality) tend to influence the design of the decision-making structure and the processes by which it is used. The particular settings and their structured connections likely to be found for admissions decisions can be predicted using these variables as informed by the Helsabeck and Kilmann models.

For example, in an institution with low or declining enrollments, there is little possibility for controlling the environment, and slack resources are difficult to come by. Information about the characteristics of the applicants for the incoming class is needed for different purposes at different levels in the organization. At the top management level, the concern is with numbers, subject to the constraint of quality, while at the faculty level, the opposite is true—the concern is with the assurance of quality, subject to the constraint of quantity. Herbert Simon's (1957) classic argument that it is meaningless to claim knowledge of an organization knowing only its manifest goals and not the constraints on them applies well here. At both institutional levels, there is a need to reduce uncertainty about the nature of the expected entering students. Hence, each group needs information that will either satisfy its decision-making requirements or assuage its anxieties.

The matrix in Figure 6.1 helps to sort out the influences on the structure. Clearly, some of the constraints/contingencies are not relevant. As the figure shows, however, size becomes a factor, driving decision making in a more centralized direction, hypothetically yielding decision making on undergraduate admissions to the top and middle management (cells 10, 11, and 13). The uncertainty of the admissions environment suggests that group coordination is likely. Thus, one might expect to find more decisions made toward the mass democratic end of the matrix—in committee or in assembly settings with participation from many (cells 11–14). On the other hand, departments tend to be autonomous, caring more for undergraduates whose interests and talents are suited to the specialized orientations regardless of the cost to the institution as a whole. Faculty and department chairs might thus be expected to participate more in the decisions (cells 20 and 21). Of course, the increased power of the administration in times of decline would point to more centralized decision making, thus putting admissions decisions more in the hands of the administration and perhaps in smaller group settings (cells 1, 2, 4, 5, and 7). Finally, the forces of collegiality might be expected to push decisions firmly into the administrative apparatus, with little or no independent faculty input (cells 16–18).

Clearly, there are not equal strengths attached to each of these influences. Indeed, the strengths oscillate as circumstances change. Faculty, for instance, are usually not concerned with undergraduate admissions at all, provided there is a history of reasonable continuity of quality. The task of undergraduate admissions falls easily to the bureaucratic side, where there is both competence to make good decisions and interest. However, if there is a threat to continuity, or if it is violated too frequently, then faculty will wish to enter the decision-making processes. Uncertainty thus strongly directs the nature of the setting in which the decisions will be made.

To summarize, the material in this chapter is intended to bring together into keener focus the variety of influences that affect the location of the authority for decision making in various domains of activity in higher education. The four categories of influence—information, coordination, power, and collegiality—exist in different strengths depending on the domain. The degree to which an institution is collegial, however, will make it easier to predict the dispersion of authority for each domain, and, indeed, for all domains together. In the next several chapters, the orientation shifts somewhat away from the institution to the faculty member as the unit of analysis of decision making. Faculty perceptions of the various influences discussed thus far will be considered.

Part Two

Individual Perceptions of Decision Making

CHAPTER SEVEN

Faculty as Judges of Decision-Making Effectiveness— A Framework

In Part 1, the presence of the common decision-making structures in higher education was explained using several of the tools of social science. In particular, the concern was with the nature of the dispersion of power and authority as a response to certain organizational needs—more precisely, information flow and coordination, and collegiality and power. It is necessary to turn now to a discussion of the effects of organizational design and power on organizational participants. Beginning in this chapter, the discussion in Part 2 moves from the organization as the unit of analysis to the organizational member—more particularly, the faculty member. Of special interest is understanding the basis of the judgments and feelings of faculty members with respect to the use of power and authority in their institutions. Faculty perspectives on the legitimacy of administrative power and authority are important clues in unraveling the puzzle of university organization and administration. In short, the phenomenological approach to understanding organizational behavior needs to be considered.

Faculty Orientations

When authority and power to control important parts of one's personal and professional lives rest in part on others, it is likely and normal that some anxiety will arise, especially when it is not clear how much trust to ascribe to those others (Zander, Cohen, & Stotland, 1959). Hence, it is a rare administrator who is viewed with equanimity by faculty members, since the former does, indeed, exercise a varying and, as maintained above, frequently uncertain amount of control over the latter. There are, however, a number of conditions that mitigate faculty anxieties about possible abuses of administrator power. Among these are the more stable, ongoing elements of organizational life—the organizational structure referred to in Chapter 1 and, potentially, the organizational culture. These elements (conceived helpfully by Kerr, 1977, and Kerr & Jermier, 1978, as "substitutes for leadership") include assumptions about the commonality of goals and values between faculty and administration; the authority structure (e.g., formal and informal constraints on the exercise of power); tradition (inviolable role boundaries of the faculty member set by tradition and organizational saga); a habitual pattern of comity in administrator-faculty relations (trust and rationality leading to collegiality); and grievance procedures known to work. There are also idiosyncratic conditions that allay faculty worries about administrator power, including the power of the individual faculty member (e.g., through his/her stature as a leader); exit and career alternatives; and, finally, the sheer force of faculty personality, which, on the one hand, may be sufficient to overwhelm the opposition or, on the other, may simply be insouciant or uncaring. Each of these represents to the faculty member either a barrier to external intrusions on his/her prerogatives or a weapon for preserving the sacred, sacrosanct, existential work value so treasured by academics—automony.

Needless to say, administrators are seen not only as potential enemies (though in times of organizational woe and travail, particularly of the economic variety, their alleged ogre-like qualities are said to predominate). Administrators do have, after all, some potential for creating conditions through which faculty can seek and find satisfactions by the efficient exercise of their professional responsibilities. Seen as resource providers, administrators are often perceived as capable of expanding the boundaries of faculty opportunity.

It is clear that "perspectives" are important in understanding the dynamics of faculty-administrator relationships. As Cameron and Whetten (1983) note, it is critical that the person from whose viewpoint effectiveness is judged be identified, particularly since organizations cannot satisfy all constituencies simultaneously. The effectiveness of administrators will be seen by faculty in ways different from the administrators' own notions; and measurement of the degree of effectiveness being exhibited will vary according to the different perspectives of faculty member and administrator. It is the purpose of the next two chapters to examine the perspectives of faculty members on administrator effectiveness, to explore the reasons for their particular conceptualizations, and to analyze the conditions that lead to their evaluation of administrator effectiveness as high or low. A better understanding of the dynamics of faculty perspectives on administrator effectiveness will permit each group to appreciate decision-making structures accurately and to modify behavior accordingly.

The Concept of Effectiveness

It is necessary first, of course, to have in mind some definition of "effectiveness." While much recent literature has been devoted to a better understanding of this concept (Cameron, 1978, 1986a, 1986b; Cameron & Whetten, 1981, 1983, 1984; Ghorpade, 1977; Goodman & Pennings, 1977; Muchinsky & Morrow, 1980; Spray, 1976; Steers, 1977), it generally identifies the total organization as the focal system. Effectiveness, in other words, is most commonly conceived of in terms of organizational achievement, particularly through success in exploiting external environments (Katz & Kahn, 1978; Yuchtman & Seashore, 1967). While the definition of effectiveness of units within organizations might use some of the same terminology, it is difficult to circumscribe the boundaries of the subsystsem (Hall & Fukami, 1979; Steers, 1975). Moreover, for our purposes here, the concern is not so much with unit effectiveness (e.g., the administrator's "office"), as with personal effectiveness (i.e., the perceived effectiveness of the person occupying the role of office leader). Clearly, there is a connection between unit or office effectiveness and personal or leadership effectiveness (Fiedler, 1967). Indeed, faculty link intimately the administrator and his/her office. There is, however, a lack of complete overlap in the conceptions of the effectiveness of leader of the office and the office itself — the latter being contingent on factors other than the administrator's competence as leader. For the purposes of the discussion in this book of judging managerial effectiveness, the idea of "personal effectiveness" (Calder, 1977) of administrators, as judged by faculty, will be used.

Viewed in this light, personal effectiveness may be seen as both behavior and personal attributes that conform to several sets of expectations of criterion populations — those persons with whom the focal person has reciprocally interdependent organizational contact (Jacobson, Charters, & Lieberman, 1951). Such expectations are typically set in the theoretical context of "systems" and "role." Faculty perceptions of the effectiveness of administrator role behavior are contingent on three aspects of the organization: (a) normative and structural conditions in the organization and its relationship to its environment; (b) characteristics of the administrator and his/her behavior; and (c) characteristics of the perceiver. Each of these and the relationships among them must be considered in some detail.

Plan of Part 2

Four related themes are pursued in Chapter 8:

> Classification of types of decisions
> Classification of types of organizations
> Identification of phases or stages of organizational evolution
> Classification of types of power and power use

and two others in Chapter 9:

> Classification of faculty by personality type
> Perspectives on effectiveness

The analysis begins in Chapter 8 from the organizational perspective with a sketch of a theory for classifying the types of decisions that must be made in all organizations. As will be noted, theoretical perspectives that have already been outlined in earlier chapters will be utilized. Because the perspectives are often complicated, they are explained again in some detail, at the risk of apparent redundancy. After consideration of the functional prerequisites of Talcott Parsons (1951) — adaptation, goal attainment, integration, and latency (AGIL), as noted in Chapter 1 — the discussion turns to a schema for understanding and/or classifying different kinds of organizations in which these prerequisites may be said to operate (presumably somewhat differently in the different kinds of organizations). As in Chapter 4, the typology of Jeffrey Pfeffer (1977) is used, thus characterizing organizations as one of four types — professional, political/coalition, bureaucratic, and centralized. Since organizations are not static — varying internally and responding to outside changes — it is necessary to classify the system states of the organization in order to understand faculty expectations. Of particular concern at this point, therefore, is the identification of the constraints of the "dominant" phase in which the organization finds itself, since the phase will predispose the administrator to adopt orientations toward others (namely, faculty) that are more characteristic of that phase (Cameron & Whetten, 1981; Parsons, 1951). The "pattern variables" of Parsons are used to explicate this phenomenon.

The analysis then turns to the kinds of power that are available to administrators and to a consideration of the conditions that make the use of one or another type appear to faculty as particularly appropriate to effect their desired ends. The power theories of Bacharach and Lawler (1980) are joined with those discussed earlier, to conclude the analysis of the organizational factors that legitimize, in faculty members' eyes, the different kinds of administrator behavior. In Chapter 9, a correlative concern — the idiographic influences on faculty perceptions of effectiveness — is examined, employing the theories of Kilmann (1977) and Kilmann and Herden (1976). The discussion allows an analysis of faculty not as a monolith, but as a disaggregated congeries of persons or subcultures with personalities predisposing them to see administrator types and administrator behavior in quite different ways. Figure 7.1 (on the next page) shows the concepts of concern in the next two chapters.

Figure 7.1
Sources of Influence on Faculty
Perceptions of Administrator Effectiveness

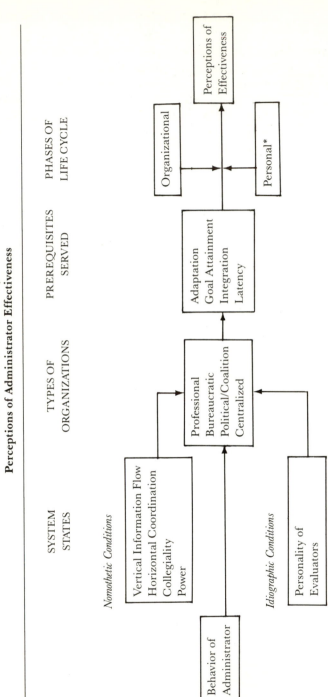

*Not considered in this chapter.

CHAPTER EIGHT

The Influence of Organizational Characteristics on Faculty Perceptions of Administrator Effectiveness

Organizations as social systems have system-level problems to which they must attend if they are to survive. These problems are universal, regardless of the type of organization. To understand the faculty perspective on administrator effectiveness, therefore, it is necessary to look first to a conceptualization of the nature of the generic problems that administrators must face. As Reid (1982) has noted, evaluation of administrators still lacks conceptual as well as empirical clarity, despite a recent increase in publications on the subject. What follows, then, is an effort to reconceive the issue of effectiveness of administrators, again borrowing heavily from the social science literature. Since there are many different kinds of administrators in higher education, for purposes of clarity the discussion here focuses on only one—the typical arts and sciences dean in a college or university.

The functionalist approach of Talcott Parsons (1960b) noted in Chapter 1 provides a useful schema for analysis. The shift back to Parsons here, rather than a continuation of the format of the four system-oriented decisions (inputs, transformation processes, outputs, and feedback), is reasonable since the Parsons schema deals more substantially with organizational affect, an important variable in perceptions of leadership effectiveness. While some may argue that any "functionalist" perspective is improperly biased toward organizational stasis, a different position is taken here, grounded in both theory and observation. The position here is that organizations with culture goals (Etzioni, 1961), such as colleges and universities, tend to be more stable systems than profit-making enterprises and to operate in a somewhat more static than dynamic equilibrium. This is not to suggest, of course, that universities and colleges do not face uncertainties in the input domain; it is only to indicate that in general their environments are more predictable and less turbulent than in the corporate sector.

According to Parsons (1960b), all social systems *qua* organizations must satisfy four prerequisites in order to ensure their long-term survival. In Figure 8.1, these prerequisites are set out theoretically in a two-by-two format, the axes of which address, on the one hand, the boundaries of the activities satisfying the prerequisites, and, on the other, the instrumental versus consummatory motivation of workers. The prerequisites are adaptation, goal attainment, integration, and latency (AGIL). If all organizations (and each of their subsystems) must meet these prerequisites, than it can be argued that to some degree organizational leadership is "responsible" for the activities associated with the prerequisites. Some part of that leadership lies with the administration. Different constituencies acting as role senders (e.g., trustees, presidents, alumni, faculty, and students), formally or informally, hold administrators accountable for their effectiveness in each area. Those with power can apply sanctions for good or bad performance; those without may form coalitions to counter the power (Gamson, 1968), register dissatisfactions through reduced performance, or undergo some psychological strain, which may also impair performance.

A further explication of the prerequisites will help clarify their importance in understanding the leader's role in addressing them. (For purposes of illustration hereinafter, the "dean" will be the leader to whom reference is made.) *Goal attainment* refers to the necessity of every organization to establish a relatively stable relation with its environment through which both the organization and environment can achieve their ends. To some extent, the environment external to

Figure 8.1
Functional Prerequisites of Organizations
According to Talcott Parsons

	INSTRUMENTAL	CONSUMMATORY
CROSS-BOUNDARY	Adaptation	Goal Attainment
INTERNAL	Latency	Integration

the organization must see the outputs of the organization as useful, and employees must derive some satisfaction from the sense of the organization's functional utility with respect to the environment. Decanal decisions addressing this prerequisite, then, would be concerned with cross-boundary conditions and with the problems of ensuring the motivational commitment of both organization and clients in the environment to the consummation of the organization's outputs (such as competent graduates, scientific research knowledge, and so forth). Curricular design, student relations, and long-range planning are administrator activities subsumed in this area.

Adaptation is a prerequisite that describes the organization's necessity to secure adequate resources from its environment and to distribute those resources internally in an efficient manner. A dean concerned with decisions satisfying this prerequisite would be occupied with recruitment of faculty, with securing and distributing funds through grants and normal budget procedures, and with ensuring an adequate supply of students.

The third prerequisite, *integration*, refers to the necessity for solidarity and mutual support among units within an organization. Members of the system must accept the roles of others and derive satisfaction from the collaborative efforts of all. A dean performing actions in this domain might spend time at faculty meetings describing and explaining the importance of various units to the overall functioning of the college. The fourth prerequisite is *latency* or pattern maintenance and tension reduction. In every organization, there must be a continuity of relationships among units. Members must be enabled to rely on expectations of patterns of activities among units. Commonly, these expectations are set in the context of an organization structure that delineates the roles of the various participants. The expectations are also determined by the normative structure or "culture" that evolves to guide behavior not covered through institutionalized role descriptions. This has been discussed earlier in the consideration of collegiality. Lacking stability of expectations, as in a highly anarchic organization, members of an organization will become tense and anxious, and their relationships with one another will become less functional for the organization. A dean concerned with this prerequisite must attend to the formalization of relationships among member units (outlining the task requirements of each), as well as to the inculcation of values and norms that guide members in institutionally desired directions where roles are diffuse or ambiguous.

Organizational Types and Administrator Performance

Having considered the system prerequisites that obtain in any organization and to which a dean must attend, it is necessary now to discuss how the satisfaction of the prerequisites might be accomplished in different kinds of organizations. Needed is a typology of organizations that will lend itself to this purpose. As noted in Chapter 1, a number of descriptive models of organization appear recurrently in the literature on higher education (e.g., Baldridge et al., 1978; Cohen & March, 1974; Millett, 1978; Mortimer & McConnell, 1978). With the exception of the Cohen and March approach, most of the models in some way employ as central parameters the concepts of goal consensus and bureaucratic structure to explain the more critical decision-making processes such as personnel, budget, and curriculum. The degree of consensus among organizational members is hypothesized in these models to predict the extent to which formal structure enters into the decision-making apparatus. If the additional contingency of consensus on the appropriate technology to be used is added to these terms, the Pfeffer typology described earlier provides a useful explanatory framework, as shown in Figure 8.2.[1] The Pfeffer model comprises four different kinds of organiza-

Figure 8.2
Typology of Organizational Forms

| | *Amount of Control Possessed by Organizational Authorities* | |
	LOW	HIGH
Consensus About Goals/ Technology (Certainty)	Professional Model (1)	Bureaucratic Model (2)
Dissensus About Goals/ Technology (Uncertainty)	Political/ Coalition Model (3)	Centralized Model (4)

Adapted from Pfeffer (1977, p. 240).

---

1. Technically, Pfeffer proffers not bureaucracy but concentration of authority as an axis in his model.

tions: professional, bureaucratic, political/coalition, and centralized.

When this framework is applied to colleges and universities, the result is a fairly reasonable explanation of some of the constraints on administrator decision making. For example, where deans and faculty agree on goals and the means to achieve them, and also agree on the need for decentralized autonomy in decision making, a "professional" type of organization arises. Under other conditions, a bureaucracy, a political/coalition, or a centralized model will best describe the system.[2] In each case, a quite different set of expectations will govern perceived and enacted roles of both dean and faculty. In turn, the criteria for assessment of the dean's effectiveness will be different. Faculty, for example, will expect different kinds of performance and power use in each of the four prerequisite directions (e.g., internal/instrumental vs. external/consummatory) from a dean operating in a bureaucracy as contrasted with a political/coalition type organization. In still other words, both the type of organization and the requisite tasks to be performed influence the mode and criteria of evaluation that faculty use with respect to the dean.

Structure and Process

To this point, organizational type and organizational prerequisites have been linked in the discussion. These concepts, however, lack the concreteness of structures and processes. It is necessary now to consider the typical structures and processes in each type of organization as each prerequisite is addressed. This added specification will provide a sounder basis for understanding the structural and processual constraints on the dean's behavior and will further clarify the behavior on which faculty make their judgments of administrator effectiveness. This section discusses four structural and processual aspects of organizations as they may characterize different types of entities. What will be shown is that because the dean's control over structure and process varies widely, ascriptions of responsibility (credit and blame) may be misdirected.

As noted in Chapter 1, "structure," according to Steers,

_____

2. These types are "pure" abstractions. In reality, in all organizations some mixture occurs (cf. Childers, 1981).

refers to the manner in which an organization organizes its human resources for goal directed activities. It is the way the human parts of an organization are fitted into relatively fixed relationships that largely define patterns of interaction, coordination, and task-oriented behavior. (1977, p. 59)

Earlier it was noted that the conception of structure used in this book stems largely from the "full" bureaucracy of Pugh, Hickson, and Hinings (1969), which highlights role standardization and formalization, centralization of authority, and impersonality of procedures. For purposes of understanding the context of decanal decision making in the four Pfeffer-type models, there is a concentration here on four important subcategories of the characteristics of centralization of authority:

> Levels in the decision-making hierarchy
> Staff/line personnel ratio
> Traditional vs. matrix form of hierarchy (i.e., single vs. multiple lines of authority)
> Control roles (e.g., administrative staff vs. faculty committees)

The first two of these are related to the issues of vertical information flow discussed in Chapter 2, while the second two are concerned with the notions discussed in Chapter 3 on the subject of horizontal needs for inter-unit coordination and with the issues raised in Chapter 6 with respect to the dispersion of authority and power. As in those chapters, the concern here is not so much with conceptions of decision making taken psychologically (i.e., with models of decision making that stem from personality theory—e.g., Driver, 1984), but with organizational processes of decision making. Decisions viewed as organizational processes also have another dimension. On the one hand, they can be policy related; on the other, issue or task specific. Policy-related decisions have a continuing impact on the behavior of organizational members largely through the redefinition of roles in organizational or job design. Task-specific decisions affect members through their impact on performance in roles already defined. The decisions of a dean include both types. For example, decisions about such matters as new criteria for promotion and tenure, policies with respect to new program formation, and guidelines for student grading all affect the faculty member's conception and execution of his/her role. Annual budget allocations, on the other hand, are one-time decisions, which are more likely to have an impact on roles that are at the margin of most faculty role behavior. That is, the role activity of most faculty will not differ significantly unless the shift in budget is so great as to constitute a change in policy.[3] A key to the understanding of how organizational processes such as decision making may affect subordinate perceptions of the effectiveness of the administrator lies in the degree to which that decision making is shared. Newer contingency theories seem to suggest that there is a "zone of conditional acceptance" — an "area in which directives, orders, decisions, and so forth may or may not be accepted, depending on the office holder's leadership behavior (or lack thereof)":

> Within this area, subordinates do not "accept" orders or directives automatically, but may do so if (1) the leader is charismatically persuasive; (2) compelling information about the need for compliance is articulated; (3) subordinates are involved in the decision process and thus feel some ownership of the objectives being sought; or, (4) an implicit bargain is struck with the leader. (Miles, 1981, pp. 177–178)

Other contingency theorists dealing with leadership theory, most notably Vroom and Yetton (1973), consider the following of importance to effective decision making: the level of expertise of the followers, the need for follower compliance, and the stake of the followers in the decision — all of which lead normatively to different kinds of decision formats in order for the decision to be effective.

Generally, the decision maker is faced with the dilemma of determining the appropriate degree of participation of subordinates. As Helsabeck noted, at one end of the continuum is a category of monocratic decisions; at the other, decisions made exclusively by subordinates; and in the middle, decisions by some combination of leader and led, and/or by middle management intermediaries. It is this decision "process" that is of central importance to the discussion here. Again, the concern is with the nature of those participative processes in the different Pfeffer-type prerequisite decisions.[4]

Whereas in Chapter 6 the alternative structures for decision making in higher education (e.g., top management alone, middle management, faculty alone) in general and the potential influences on those structures were discussed, here it is important to deal more

---

3. It is, of course, conceivable that gradual increments or decrements in budgets will, over time, constitute real, if unarticulated, changes in policy (Lindblom, 1959; Hardy et al., 1984).

4. Both actual and perceived participation in each condition affect subordinate evaluations of administrator effectiveness (Calder, 1977).

concretely with the positioning of these units in the formal authority structure. That is, the distribution of authority across these structures and their influence as independent (rather than dependent) variables on the various constituencies in the institution must be discerned. In Table 8.1, the structural and decision process variables that might be considered for each of the organizations in the Pfeffer model for each of the prerequisite activities have been noted.

Obviously the utility of this schematic depiction of the structures and processes waits for empirical research to describe reliably the actual conditions in these kinds of organizations. Table 8.1 is intended to draw attention to variables that should be considered in the analysis. It is possible to speculate, moreover, on some of the patterns that might occur. In Table 8.2, the structure and participative processes that might obtain in different organizations are hypothesized, as are the probable behaviors of a dean acting out one of his/her roles. For purposes of illustration, only one of the prerequisite decisions—in the "goal-attainment" area, manifested as curriculum change—is shown.

Quite apart from the different strategies that a dean might adopt in different organizations, what is significant to observe from the hypothetical actions noted in each cell in Table 8.1 is the variation in the structural entities that serve the goal-attainment functions. As Parsons suggests with respect to the society as a whole, a different structural subsystem emerges to serve each functional prerequisite (cf. Lyden, 1975). Parsons (1960b) indicates, for example, that the adaptation function in society is served largely by the economy, while the latency function is served by such structures as schools and religious institutions. Note that in Table 8.1, the same function, organizational goal attainment, is served by quite different structural subsystems under the five model organizations. In the professional organization, it is served by line personnel—the faculty. In the bureaucratic organization, it is the dean's staff that attends to the function, while in the political organization, the department chairs and other powerful persons do the work. In the centralized college or university, the dean acts as the structure that serves the function.

This important shift in responsibility for the goal-attainment function has implications for the understanding of faculty judgments of administrator effectiveness. Since goal attainment (and, equally important, latency) is a "consummatory" function, the ascription or attribution of success to the person or persons responsible will depend on the degree to which lower participants in the organization, such as faculty or administrative staff, see the activity as gratificatory. If the dean is not directly identified as the responsible subsystem, it is quite likely that a major source of appreciation for his/her effectiveness will not be salient to faculty in their judgments of effectiveness. Indeed, this misapprehension of the sources of power and responsibility has been alluded to elsewhere as the "myth of the receding locus of power" (Lindquist & Blackburn, 1974). As will be seen later, there is associated with each phase of organizational movement on "appropriate" or effective leadership orientation or pattern variable. Cameron and Whetten note, for example, that "the criteria of institutional effectiveness applicable in one stage of development are not necessarily appropriate in other stages of development" (1984, p. 56; see also Cameron & Whetten, 1981).

Normally, it would be expected that effective leadership requires a proper matching of style and contingencies (Fiedler, 1967; Vroom, 1984). Consequently, when organizational type (per Pfeffer) is included as a contingency, and subsystems other than the leader's have primary responsibility for carrying out critical functions, the identification of an effective leader style may require a reconceptualization of the "system" toward which the leader is and must be oriented. The leadership functions of the dean, that is, may be much more circumscribed in some types of institutions than is usually believed. Faculty evaluation of decanal effectiveness must, in turn, realistically consider these more limited domains of responsibility.

The Use of Power

Not only are the mechanisms of organizational action (structure and process) different across function and organizational type, but the modes of influence over compliance of others also vary. Administrators, such as deans, exercise their influence over their organizations and their subordinates, peers, and superordinates in a variety of ways. In this section, the concern is especially with the ways in which the deans in the different types of organizations in the Pfeffer model attend to their leadership responsibilities through the use of power. Using power typologies described in earlier chapters, it is possible to examine how power is likely to be distributed in the four types of organizations, how it is exercised (using an adaptation of the Parsonian pattern variables), and whether it is perceived by faculty as effective.

As noted at the outset of this chapter, in most social systems, resistance to authority and power stems from anxiety over possible

(*Continued on page 146*)

Table 8.1
Salient Structural and Process Variables in a Cross-Tabulation Array of Organizational Types and Functional Prerequisites

TYPE OF ORGANIZATION	FUNCTIONAL PREREQUISITES (from Parsons)							
	Goal Attainment		Adaptation		Integration		Latency	
	S*	P†	S	P	S	P	S	P
Goal Consensus Types (Certain Technology)								
1. Professional Organization (low control by authorities)	DML = S/L = T-M = LRR =	DMP =	DML = S/L = T-M = LRR =	DMP =	DML = S/L = T-M = LRR =	DMP =	DML = S/L = T-M = LRR =	DMP =
2. Bureaucratic (high) control by authorities	DML = S/L = T-M = LRR =	DMP =	DML = S/L = T-M = LRR =	DMP =	DML = S/L = T-M = LRR =	DMP =	DML = S/L = T-M = LRR =	DMP =
Goal Dissensus Types (Uncertain Technology)								
3. Political/Coalition (low control by authorities)	DML = S/L = T-M = LRR =	DMP =	DML = S/L = T-M = LRR =	DMP =	DML = S/L = T-M = LRR =	DMP =	DML = S/L = T-M = LRR =	DMP =

4. Centralized (high control by authorities)	DMP = DML = S/L = T-M = LRR =	DMP = DML = S/L = T-M = LRR =	DMP = DML = S/L = T-M = LRR =	DMP = DML = S/L = T-M = LRR =
Ambiguous Goals & Technology Type 5. Anarchic (ambiguous control)	DMP = DML = S/L = T-M = LRR =	DMP = DML = S/L = T-M = LRR =	DMP = DML = S/L = T-M = LRR =	DMP = DML = S/L = T-M = LRR =

Note: See Table 8.2 for a sample of a cell from this table with the right sides of the equations filled in.

*S = Structures; †P = Process

Key to cell entries:

DML (Number of decision-making levels in the hierarchy) = H (High), M (Medium), L (Low)

S/L (Staff to line personnel ratio) = S/l (High staff to line), s/l (Moderate staff to line), s/L (High line to staff)

T-M (Traditional vs. matrix form of hierarchy) = T (Traditional, single line of authority), M (Matrix, multiple line of authority)

LRR (Linking role responsibility) = S (Staff predominates), S/L (Mixed responsibility), L (Line predominates [e.g., faculty committees])

DMP (Decision-making process) = A (Autocratic), A/L (Shared), L (Line dominated)

Table 8.2

**Hypothetical Description of Decanal Activity in the
Goal-Attainment Area in Different Types of Organizations**

	FUNCTIONAL PREREQUISITES			
TYPE OF ORGANIZATION	*Goal Attainment*	*Adaptation*	*Integration*	*Latency*
	(e.g., curriculum)	(e.g., budget)	(e.g., coordination)	(e.g., personnel evaluation)
1. *Professional Organization* DML = Flat hierarchy S/L = High line to staff T–M = Matrix LRR = Line predominates DMP = Line dominated	Dean asks faculty senate to instruct its curriculum committee to consider a new program			
2. *Bureaucratic Organization* DML = Tall hierarchy S/L = High staff to line T–M = Traditional LRR = Staff predominates DMP = Autocratic	Dean asks his/her own staff to develop a proposal to be submitted to the faculty on the subject of a new program			

3. *Political/Coalition Organization*
   DML = Medium hierarchy
   S/L = Moderate line to staff
   T-M = Traditional
   LRR = Line predominates
   DMP = Line dominated

   Dean meets with key department chairpersons to sound them out on the possibility of a new program. Dean seeks to establish coalitions with powerful faculty. Tests bargaining position with different constituencies

4. *Centralized Organization*
   DML = Tall hierarchy
   S/L = High staff to line
   T-M = Traditional
   LRR = Mixed responsibility
   DMP = Autocratic

   Dean announces new program to staff and faculty. Dean asks relevant personnel to implement program

5. *Anarchic Organization*
   DML = Ambiguous
   S/L = Ambiguous
   T-M = Ambiguous

   Dean aggregates forces indicating curricular problem and solution to problem if and when circumstances make it opportune

loss of control. Faculty, who have strong needs for autonomy, are particularly sensitive to potential intrusions on their freedom to determine not only their work schedules but the conduct of the work itself. Though they may recognize the primacy of institutional goals in organizations (Parsons, 1960b), they prefer to elect to apportion their time in accordance with their own predilections, with the hope that there is a coincidence of personality and organizational goals. Faculty perception of loss of control is mitigated by the structural conditions, decision-making processes, and organizational culture, especially collegiality as defined above, that the faculty member expects on employment or learns to tolerate during the early socialization period of employment. Not only do these set limits on faculty prerogatives, but they also define administrative action boundaries.

Regardless of type of organization, however, there is always an asymmetry of power and authority between lower- and higher-level participants. Clearly, in professional type organizations, there is a more balanced distribution, but even there, authority rests ultimately with fiduciaries. In each of the types in the Pfeffer model, there is a strain toward individual and aggregate self-control by lower participants, which may be assuaged by judicious management by the formal authorities through the promulgation of a generalized belief in the "rationality" (or legitimacy) of the processes of participation in decision making, however widely or narrowly spread. As leaders attend to the functional prerequisite of pattern maintenance, they seek to institutionalize the organizational decision-making structures that purportedly lead to the attainment of goals. Parsons refers to this as a "strain toward consistency."

Inevitably, some part of this legitimation process involves the use of political processes. As Pfeffer (1981) observes:

> In the political processes within organizations, the task of the various political actors is to develop explanations, rationalizations, and legitimation for the desired activities and choices which are themselves frequently resolved through the use of power. (p. 181)
>
> Political actors provide justifications and rationalizations that justify proposed decisions. These justifications serve to ensure support both inside the organization and from external groups, in that they are consistent with social norms, values, and expectations for organizational activity. (p. 182)

As noted earlier, administrators in different types of organizations exercise their power in different ways, each of which may or may not fit faculty expectations of appropriateness in the satisfaction of either organizational or personal prerequisites.[5] That is, the manner by which the dean defines the participative system in, say, a professional or political/coalition type organization and the ways he/ she introduces and forwards substantive matters are critical to the faculty perception of effectiveness. One way of conceiving of administrator behavior under these differing conditions is to look at the influence processes in which administrators engage (Carzo & Yanouzas, 1967, pp. 197ff).

It is useful to repeat here the classification system of Bacharach and Lawler (1980) noted in earlier chapters. These authors have suggested that power as such a process can be divided analytically into "sources," "types," and "bases," as is shown in Figure 8.3. By sources, these authors mean the modes by which actors exercise their power. Bases of power distinguish between the zero-sum and non-zero-sum (i.e., continuous) and/or formal and informal manifestations of power, while types of power refer to the currency employed in power use (e.g., money or information).

As Bacharach and Lawler note, "coercive power" is the control of punishment; "remunerative power," the control of rewards; "normative power," the control of symbols; and "knowledge power," the control of information. While some previous research on the use of power by administrators in higher education has been conducted (Bachman, 1968; Coltrin & Glueck, 1977; Cope, 1973; Hill & French, 1967; Neumann, 1978), the literature does not deal explicitly with the concept of administrator effectiveness from the faculty perspective. The value of the Bacharach and Lawler conceptualization is that it permits a diagnostic understanding of what kinds of power are likely to be used, under what conditions, and to what effect. For example, there will be different power sources, types, and bases in different organizations depending on the degree to which

---

5. The reference here is not to the concept of "satisfaction." Though a large volume of literature deals with the relationship between leader behavior and subordinate satisfaction (particularly in the "job facets" tradition), and though there is doubtless a strong relationship between satisfaction and biases in the evaluation of the superordinate by the subordinate, the attempt here is to restrict the analysis to the faculty's "impression" of administrator performance. The faculty, in other words, are considered here apart from their own satisfactions with a variety of features in their work and organizational environments (cf. Neumann, 1978; Bess, 1973b). Effectiveness judgments of faculty as they are affected by power used by administrators turn largely on the perceived legitimacy of the particular combination of power source, type, and base employed in service of a functional prerequisite in a distinctive kind of institution.

Figure 8.3
Relationships of Sources, Types,
and Bases of Power

SOURCE	TYPE	BASES
Structure	Authority	Coercion Remunerative Normative Knowledge
Personality	Influence	Normative Knowledge
Expertise	Influence	Normative Knowledge
Opportunity	Influence	Coercion Knowledge

Adapted from Bacharach and Lawler (1980, p. 36).

faculty perceive themselves as more or less dependent on decanal decisions and/or have lower or higher stakes in them.

For example, refer again to Table 8.1 and to the illustration of curriculum planning in Table 8.2, in which deans are attending to goal-attainment functions in a political/coalition type organization.[6] One could argue reasonably that in this kind of organization deans would use at least three bases of power—knowledge, remunerative, and coercion—but would find normative power (manipulation of symbols) a rather impotent base. Coercion as a base might stem from their formal "authority" in the given "structure" of the organization, although in a university with many tenured faculty, coercion may have limited effectiveness.

Remunerative power would also be derived from the position structure. Here, deans would promise—or more likely imply—the increased availability of rewards if the chairpersons agreed to curriculum revisions desired by the deans. It is equally likely, however, that deans will seek to exercise power through influence, rather than authority. Hence, they will take advantage of personality and oppor-

---

6. As will be quite obvious, because of the absence of empirical data, hypotheses on the source, type, and base of power used in this instance are speculative, to say the least.

tunity. Charismatic leadership, for example, may induce some department chairs to comply, and the particulars of the curriculum change may provide opportunities for deans to work their influence through friendship networks already established in the organization. It is not likely, however, that expertise as a source of influence will be invoked, since deans will probably not possess any superior knowledge or skills in curriculum building to which they can lay claim. Indeed, it could be argued that expertise over curriculum matters rests more solidly among the faculty — or, perhaps more importantly, is perceived to reside there.

From the faculty perspective in this type of organization, such decanal activity would probably be viewed as legitimate and effective, even by those faculty members who are the losers in the political battles for control over their working lives. In another type of organization, say the "professional" type identified in the Pfeffer model, it would not, particularly since a different "structure" serving the goal-attainment prerequisite predominates here. In the case of a professional type organization, it might be hypothesized (again quite speculatively) that a different pattern of power sources, types, and bases would be employed. It is reasonable to expect a much heavier reliance on normative and knowledge bases, with coercion and remunerative bases less operative. In common with the political/coalition type organization, deans would rely on personality and opportunity to influence the faculty and, again, expertise would be subordinated.

It is important to reiterate that a dean's authority and/or influence, potential or actual, refer not only to the substance of curriculum change (or any other matter), but also to the process itself. Thus, decanal power will be exerted in directions meant either to legitimize the decision-making process (the "governance" mechanism in postsecondary institutions) or to subvert it — depending on the type of organization. For example, whereas constitutionally in universities the faculty may have "authority" over curriculum matters, deans in political/coalition university organizations may attempt through power to undermine that authority, and in professional/collegial organizations, they may strive to support its legitimacy. Importantly, in each case, faculty may see the activity, when it is successful, as both legitimate and "effective." Indeed, to the extent that deans conform to these faculty expectations, faculty will view them as furthering the faculty's objectives and are likely themselves to act in ways congruent with the dean's (and presumably the organization's) goals (House, 1971).

Organizational Life-Cycle Phases

At this point, one more contingency must be added to the predictions of faculty assessment of administrator effectiveness. Earlier, it was suggested that evaluations of effectiveness are related to the time frame in which the objectives of the administrator are to be accomplished. Here, another time-related dimension of organizational politics must be noted. As organizations proceed through various cycles of development, change, decline, and rejuvenation (Kimberly, Miles, & Associates, 1980; Cameron & Whetten, 1984), more or less attention is paid to one or another of the prerequisites (Parsons, Bales, & Shils, 1953; Mintzberg, 1984; Cobb, 1984). In Parsons' terms, these "phases" are changing states of the system through some interval of time, when, in ipsative fashion, more organizational energy is addressed to one prerequisite at the expense of the others. Most important for the discussion here is the assertion by Parsons that in each phase, there are dominant modes of orientations of the actors in the system and dominant modalities or meanings that the actors attach to others in the system. Both orientations and modalities constitute what Parsons (1953, 1960) calls the "pattern variables," each of which has four possible values.

The modes of orientation describe the systematic, patterned ways that actors in social systems such as organizations have interests in or are related to other persons or objects in the systems. Parsons (1951) suggests that one can categorize the interests in others in social situations through two dichotomous variables — (1) the degree to which the actor desires a "specific" vs. a more "diffuse" relationship; and (2) the degree to which the actor wants to become involved in and derive satisfaction from relationships ("affectivity") vs. the desire to remain "neutral" toward others.[7] For example, an actor such as a faculty member or dean may see others in instrumental terms (specificity–neutrality) — in other words, how others can be of assistance in forwarding his/her own ends. Another example might be a dean who sees a particular faculty member as a source of personal satisfaction (specificity–affectivity). Hills (1968) illustrates the alternatives in a two-by-two figure (Figure 8.4).

The "modalities" or categories of *meaning* to the actor are also subject to dichotomous classification (Hills, 1968, p. 5). Another two-by-two figure (Figure 8.5) describes these categories. To give one

---

7. These terms are clearly related to the conceptualization of "c-collegiality" in Chapter 5.

Figure 8.4
Modes of Orientation

	NEUTRALITY	AFFECTIVITY
SPECIFICITY	Need for Instrumental Utilization	Need for Consummation
DIFFUSENESS	Need for Commitment	Need for Solidarity

illustration, highly research-oriented faculty members might view deans largely in terms of universalism and performance—that is, solely in terms of what deans (irrespective of their personalities or special context of action) can do in the role.

As noted above, distinctive orientations and modalities can be seen to be operative in each of the phases. In what follows, the concern is with the ways in which the phase of the organization affects deans' orientations toward faculty as the deans' roles are executed politically in each of the types of organization identified earlier. The focus will also be on how these different attitudes in different phases affect faculty interpretation of the effectiveness of the deans.

There are five kinds of pattern variables, one of which is not relevant here. Only one of the remaining four will be seen to suffuse the orientations of the actors each time one or another prerequisite becomes dominant. The particular orientations that obtain when any one of the prerequisites is salient are noted in Figure 8.6. While all of the phase orientations cannot be illustrated here because of space limitations, one will be used as an example. Most colleges and universities in the late 1980s must be especially attentive to accommodating the institution to changing environmental conditions. Such a situation requires an active concern for the structural and

Figure 8.5
Modalities of Meaning

	UNIVERSALISM	PARTICULARISM
PERFORMANCE	Objects of Utility	Goal Objects
QUALITY	Objects of Generalized Respect	Objects of Identification

Figure 8.6
Pattern Variable Characteristics of the
Functional Prerequisites

ADAPTATION	Specificity (vs. Diffuseness)
	Universalism (vs. Particularism)
GOAL ATTAINMENT	Affectivity (vs. Affective Neutrality)
	Performance (vs. Quality)
LATENCY	Affective Neutrality (vs. Affectivity)
	Quality (vs. Performance)
INTEGRATION	Diffuseness (vs. Specificity)
	Particularism (vs. Universalism)

Adapted from Bess (1971, p. 83).

processual changes in the organization needed to attend to new external conditions. In the conception of Parsons, Bales, and Shils (1953), this new orientation is reflective of an increased concentration on the successful satisfaction of the adaptation prerequisite:

> The eventual mastery of the external situation through instrumental activity necessitates "realistic" judgments in terms of generalized predictions concerning the behavior of objects. Hence, the relation of actors to objects needs to be universalistic, that is, cognizant of the characteristics of the object in relation to other objects' characteristics. It is necessary, moreover, if the situation is to be "mastered" and not simply "accommodated to" for these universalistically defined properties to be perceived and dealt with in specific contexts of relevance to given goal-interests. Hence the character of the attitude tends to be marked by specificity of interest. (p. 183)

Translated into more practical terms, these authors can be interpreted as suggesting that when organizations under stress become more concerned with successfully mastering their adaptation to external and internal changes (e.g., reduced numbers of applications from students), the actors in those organizations tend to become more performance-oriented and to view others in the organization from a more cognitive perspective. Thus, it is possible to understand why quantitative criteria are becoming more important in admissions evaluations. Moreover, affective or emotional reactions are inhibited, since those attitudes tend to be more appropriate to the activities required in other prerequisites. Perhaps most important for the argument here is the observation that for some types of organizations, there may be a time lag between the recognition of administrators and the awareness of faculty that the organization has moved into a new phase. Hence, faculty tend to expect the predominant orientations of a prior phase and are not prepared for the shift to the new orientations. In terms of rated effectiveness of administrators, therefore, faculty will apply standards that are "out of phase" with the needs of the institution as a whole. As will be shown, however, not all types of organizations are as subject to changes in decision-making climates and modes as others.

This can be illustrated by again referring to the three organizing principles discussed thus far: type of organization (Pfeffer), prerequisite (Parsons), and power (Bacharach & Lawler). Deans attending to a curriculum decision (goal-attainment prerequisite) in political type organizations that were experiencing a relatively affluent period might use knowledge, remuneration, and coercion, as noted earlier. As Figure 8.6 indicates, however, the dominant orientation of actors in goal-attainment decisions (and in organizations whose phase is weighted toward goal attainment) is "affectivity" and "performance." The norms of the organization and the politics of the situations, then, require the deans' activities to be framed in terms of affectivity and performance. They must relate to faculty in expressive ways and must symbolize achievements of the unit of organization in very concrete terms so that their meanings can be appreciated or "consumed" by the faculty. The political modes commonly employed in political type organizations do not, however, lend themselves to such decanal orientations. The result is the formation of various informal coalitions and the suboptimization of goals by formal units, partially as accommodations to the prescribed behavior of the formal leader. Too, as noted above, other subsystems than the dean's office may be called upon to serve the goal-attainment function.

If, on the other hand, the same type of organization — political — under a different phase, say in a period of decline, is considered, the dominant mode can be characterized as "adaptation." Here the expectation is that the deans' orientations toward faculty will reflect specificity and universalism. In this case, the political power source, type, and base more closely "fit" the expectation. In part, this explains the orientations of actors in many political type organizations.

There is a strain to treat the system as having an economy of scarcity, even when resources are ample. (See the discussion in Chapter 1 of Hardin's tragedy of the commons.) The proclivity stems from the inertia of the organization's political ethos or saga, which, in turn, requires a continual legitimation of the modes of decision making extant. In short, an organization once politicized tends to remain so (Nadler, Hackman, & Lawler, 1979, p. 227; Pfeffer, 1981, p. 32). The "phase," then, in a political type organization may not be as critical to the faculty's evaluation of the dean's effectiveness.

Such is probably not the case in another of the Pfeffer-type organizations. This can be illustrated by examining, more briefly, a "professional" organization. In such an organization, there is a high degree of consensus about goals and about the means of achieving them, as well as agreement about the legitimacy of decentralization of authority. In a goal-attainment phase, occasioned by slack resources, the dean of a professional organization would be likely to rely on influence rather than authority as the type of power and on personality and opportunity as sources of power (see Table 8.2). (Again, expertise as a source would be unlikely, since faculty might be expected to have more knowledge in curriculum matters than would a dean unfamiliar with a particular field.) While coercion as a power base would be unlikely, the deans might use special knowledge gained opportunistically in their positions and would use and manipulate norms to effect the changes they desire.

In a phase dominated by goal attainment, it might be predicted (according to Parsons) that the orientation of actors would be dominated by affectivity (vs. affective neutrality) and performance (vs. quality)—see Figure 8.6. Deans, for example, concerned with demonstrating the consummatory character of the organization's achievements, would find themselves willing to express their affective orientation. They would see the achievements as unique performances of faculty and not as manifestations of static work expectations. In good times, then, in a professional organization, faculty would be responsive to decanal behavior of this sort. Here again, there is a "fit," as there was for the political type organization in the adaptation phase. Moreover, as noted earlier, in a professional type organization, the structural subsystem primarily responsible for the goal-attainment activity is the faculty itself, not the dean's office, so questions of maladaptation or misfit are not critical.

In times of decline, on the other hand, when the adaptation phase predominates, the expectation is that persons in this (as in the political) organization will be dominated by specificity (vs. diffuseness) and universalism (vs. particularism) in the interests of attending to the instrumental nature of activities concerned with adaptation. While deans in professional type organizations would still rely on knowledge and normative power bases, they would relate to each faculty achievement primarily as a means to an organizational end, not as a pleasurable source of cathexis, for either the dean or faculty member. In contrast to the goal-attainment function, deans and their offices are the subsystem seen to be responsible for adaptation. Hence, faculty members will look to deans for leadership.

An important distinction must be made here between faculty as line workers and faculty as managers (Etzioni, 1961). Insofar as faculty perform the basic work activities of research and teaching, they view deans according to their capacity to facilitate those processes. In their managerial functions, on the other hand, the subsystem of faculty views deans as colleagues or competitors for power and authority, depending on the particular type of organization. In an adaptation phase, faculty in a professional type organization may find their resources for performing their line functions reduced. In this case, they will tend to be oriented toward deans from the same perspective as the deans are toward them — that is, in terms of specificity and universalism. They will see deans and their offices as instruments serving them. They will consider deans specifically as a means of providing resources and will have expectations that those resources will be provided without bias. Since the model of a professional type organization requires that both faculty and dean be committed to the decentralization of power, faculty will continue, even as the organization shifts from a goal-attainment phase to an adaptation phase, to serve as the subsystem responsible for goal attainment and, in its managerial capacity, for adaptation. It is entirely possible, then, that the dean in such an organization would serve more as a figurehead than an executive. Faculty evaluations of the dean's effectiveness apparently are not affected by the efficacy of the dean in either of these two crucial functional prerequisites. Rather, the dean will be viewed as effective to the extent that he/she serves the two internal prerequisites of integration and pattern maintenance. The phase through which the professional organization is passing, then, is also not critical to the evaluation of the dean's effectiveness. In other kinds of organizations (e.g., bureaucratic and centralized), on the other hand, faculty will tend to be much more sensitive to phase movements, with concomitant shifts in responsibility for prerequisite functions and changes in expected behaviors and attitudes of organizational actors.

The Ambiguity of Structure and Phase

The Pfeffer four-fold organizational schema speaks in part to the issue of governance in institutions of higher education, but the definition of "authority" is complicated in this field, particularly at the higher end of the institutional complexity scale. As was pointed out in the Introduction and in Chapter 6, the more complex the institution, the more authority for the execution of different functions is spread traditionally across both administrative and faculty personnel settings. Moreover, with complexity there arises an increasing diffuseness in the boundaries of decision making — a diffuseness having both functional and dysfunctional consequences. The organization under these conditions inevitably becomes more politicized, even when there is consensus on goals and technology but especially when consensus is absent, as in the other two Pfeffer categories of institution. Trust and rationality are less likely when there are unclear or multiple goals and when there is an uncertain technology.

What is critical to understand here is that whereas the functions identified by Parsons must still be satisfied, the authority structures in complex institutions like universities are often ambiguous (Cohen & March, 1974). While faculty handbooks and constitutions frequently identify what seem to be clear-cut jurisdictional authority domains, in reality, decisions are often made *sub rosa* either by dominant coalitions of faculty or by faculty and key administrators working toward common goals, which may not be those of the majority (Cyert & March, 1963; Mortimer & McConnell, 1979). Under these varying conditions of institutional differentiation, the role of the dean thus may shift frequently from administrative manager to political leader and back. As this occurs, faculty expectations of the dean also shift. As Ryan notes:

> Organizational members may hold one set of expectations for the dean's role in the administrative organization and another set for his role in the academic organization. While the two structures appear to serve different institutional functions and thus be conceptually independent, in practice there may be a blurring of responsibilities. (1980, p. 142)

Perhaps most interesting in this ambiguity is a concomitant shifting of faculty orientations from concerns with the administrator's effectiveness in creating organizational conditions that permit faculty members to maximize their ego satisfactions (via teaching or research) to the administrator's effectiveness in maximizing the faculty members' lower-order needs — such as for job continuity (e.g., tenure) and financial security and well-being. To follow the Parsons framework (using the "person" as the system), faculty members will shift from attempts to satisfy the consummatory prerequisites (goal attainment and integration) to efforts addressing the instrumental prerequisites (adaptation and pattern maintenance and tension reduction). With this change in orientation come changes in expectations of decanal behavior.

When faculty are oriented toward deans who act as political leaders in an academic governance structure characterized by shared power and decision making with respect to organizational goal attainment or the integration of units, they expect quite different behavior and attitudes than when they see the dean as an evaluator of their prospects for tenure or salary advancement. As Hills notes:

> From the system phase perspective, we may say that (1) if the primary functional problem of the system is adaptation (the production of generalized facilities) the actors are expected to adhere to norms which incorporate the universalistic categorization of objects and specificity of interest; (2) if the primary functional problem of the system is the attainment of a goal for the system, then actors are expected to adhere to norms which incorporate performance categorization of objects and affective interest; (3) if the primary functional problem of the system is integration, then actors are expected to adhere to norms defined in terms of particularism and diffuseness; and (4) if the primary functional problem of the system is pattern-maintenance, then actors are expected to adhere to norms which call for quality categorization of objects and neutral basis of interest. (1968, p. 30)

In other words, when deans act to make decisions on how the institution can better achieve its goals (e.g., through curriculum change), faculty norms permit them to categorize and define the nature of the proposal concretely and specifically to indicate its probable effects, and to express openly their feelings about the matter. On the other hand, when deans act in an evaluative function, faculty expect norms of quality and neutrality. As noted above, as organizations fluctuate in phases requiring attention to different prerequisites, there is a lag in the "appropriate" shift in faculty expectations of decanal performance and an accompanying confusion over whether the dean can be judged an effective administrator.

What is important to recognize here is that normative gaps in the organizational culture, particularly in complex, political/coalition type institutions, result in ambiguity about the nature of authority over different kinds of decisions. Often it is easier to determine what the structure of decision making is than to assess its practicality, especially when the institution is in transition to a different phase. As a result, faculty members must themselves interpret both. Since such interpretation may not be accurate, there arises an inevitable potential for erroneous evaluation of the dean's effectiveness, and a corresponding propensity for dissatisfaction, however unjustified.

In this chapter, the aim has been to determine the organizational influences on faculty perceptions of administrative effectiveness. In the next chapter, a contrasting basis for faculty interpretations of administrator effectiveness will be presented—namely, the idiographic, which is based on the aggregate of the personalities of faculty in different subcultures.

CHAPTER

NINE The Influence of Personal
Characteristics
on Faculty Perspectives
of Power and Authority

In Chapter 8, the dean's relationship to the faculty was examined from the perspective of the variation in organizational characteristics. A simplifying assumption was made there that "the faculty" could be viewed holistically — as a monolith. From research evidence and practical experience, however, we know that such is not the case. Faculty differ not only individually but in manifest and latent identities and orientations (Lazarsfeld & Thielens, 1958; Bess, 1982; Biglan, 1973; Gouldner, 1957,1958; Ladd & Lipset, 1975; Trow, 1975; Thompson, Hawkes, & Avery, 1969; Kelly & Hart, 1971; Peters, 1979; Smart & Elton, 1975; Smart & McLaughlin, 1978; Finkelstein, 1981). Hence, it is necessary to partition the faculty in ways that help in understanding the differential perceptions of administrator effectiveness held by faculty of different persuasions. Doing this will permit the dean a better appreciation of the strategies and tactics that best match the largest number of faculty leadership style preferences. It is, of course, unlikely that any administrator will always be able to satisfy all faculty members all the time (just as Mann & Associates, 1970, found that no teacher could maximize his/her effectiveness all the time, given the diversity of students in a classroom).

There is a very large number of ways in which faculty can be divided. The most common are into the traditional disciplines and schools. Much research points to the differences in psychological orientations that obtain across faculty in different fields. Hence, to some extent, faculty appraisals of administrator effectiveness will be a function of the similarities in disciplinary backgrounds between the faculty and administrator. If a managerial style is associated with a dean's personality, then it would seem to follow that faculty with similar personality dispositions would tend to find the dean's style more acceptable and might in turn be predisposed to find his/her actions more effective.

To disaggregate the faculty in a university in the most parsimonious way requires a return to the typology introduced in Chapter 1 — namely, the classification of individual orientations or dispositions according to "psychological type." This is a construct built on Jungian archetypes, though here only parts of the theory are utilized. A brief review of the approach will be useful before considering how it may apply to university settings.

According to the theory, people are disposed to consider information they receive (the first dimension) according to one of two personality functions: sensation or intuition. Sensation is a perceptual orientation that focuses on details and facts, particularly in a "now" orientation to situations. Intuition, on the other hand, has a holistic, global character and occurs when people tend to use hunches, imagination, and futuristic means of understanding phenomena.

In processing data received (making decisions based on them — the second dimension), people are disposed to use one of two other personality functions: thinking or feeling. Thinking "is the judgmental function concerned with formulating impersonal rules, logical procedures, and analytical approaches for making decisions," while "feeling as judgment is concerned with extreme individual cases and with personal and subjective value judgments for decision making" (Kilmann & Herden, 1976). Kilmann and Herden call these two dimensions the "input data dimension" and the "decision-making dimension," respectively. When each perception function is combined with each judgment function, four psychological types are created, as can be seen in Figure 9.1. Individuals who fall into these four categories tend to define and solve problems in quite different ways. Kilmann and Herden go on to suggest that the goals of per-

Figure 9.1
Psychological Types Created
from Perception and Judgment Functions

INPUT DATA DIMENSION	DECISION-MAKING DIMENSION	
	Thinking (T)	Feeling (F)
Sensation (S)	ST	SF
Intuition (N)	NT	NF

sons evaluating the effectiveness of others vary according to the psychological type into which they fall. Kilmann and Herden (1976; cf. Mitroff & Kilmann, 1978) have suggested that "evaluators will process information in a way that is congruent with the perception component of their personalities." Moreover, "they will formulate a conceptual model for the evaluation, based upon their perceptions and congruent with the judgment component of their personalities."

The authors note that sensation-thinking personalities (STs) tend to be concerned with "internal efficiency" or the establishment of optimum levels of quantity, quality, and efficiency. Faculty with this orientation, then, would expect deans to be superior in maximizing the ratio of outputs to inputs. "Good" deans for this group would be concerned, for example, with making sure that student and faculty interaction in and out of class was carefully planned, organized, and directed.

Intuition-thinking faculty (NTs), on the other hand, would look at deans in terms of the latter's overall effectiveness in securing adequate resources for them, either from the central administration (through shrewd bargaining) or through the facilitation of grant proposal writing. These types of faculty, in other words, would view deans as effective when the latter fought successfully for resources on their behalf or created imaginative new programs that could be funded. Sensation-feeling faculty (SFs) take another approach to evaluation, looking for detailed facts but putting highly personal judgments on those facts, particularly as they affect interpersonal relations. Good deans in the opinion of these faculty members are ones who can create a trusting, close-knit, collegial community of scholars who truly care for one another as individuals. They are also able to address each faculty member individually and are successful in attending to the faculty member's deeper sources of motivation.

Finally, the intuition-feeling faculty members (NFs) take a broader view of the problems of human society, viewing their organizational lives "through the gestalt, by synthesis and personalistic value judgment" (Kilmann & Herden, 1976). Effective deans for this group would be those who successfully led their colleges to significant improvements in the society outside the institution.

The four different perspectives on evaluation of deans are set in the context of internal–external orientations and effectiveness and efficiency, according to Kilmann and Herden. Their model, with some modifications, appears in Figure 9.2. (A similar model appears in Figure 1.3.) The similarity of this typology to that of Parsons appears to be accidental (no reference to Parsons appears in the

Figure 9.2
A Model of Organizational Effectiveness

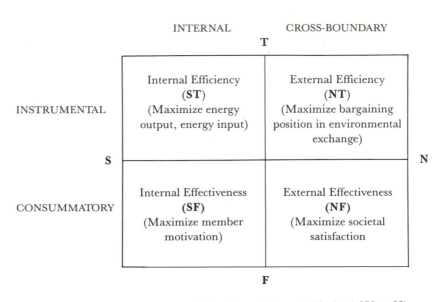

INTERNAL   CROSS-BOUNDARY

T

	Internal Efficiency **(ST)** (Maximize energy output, energy input)	External Efficiency **(NT)** (Maximize bargaining position in environmental exchange)
INSTRUMENTAL		
CONSUMMATORY	Internal Effectiveness **(SF)** (Maximize member motivation)	External Effectiveness **(NF)** (Maximize societal satisfaction

S   N

F

Adapted from Kilmann & Herden (1976, p. 92).

Kilmann & Herden bibliography), but it is striking nevertheless. What it suggests is the STs will be concerned primarily with integration, NTs with adaptation, SFs with latency, and NFs with goal attainment. Perhaps more important, as the organization proceeds through different phases, any one dean will be successively matched and mismatched with the phase, since the dean's own personality disposition itself falls into one or another of the Jungian categories. Hence, the faculty's evaluation of the dean will be made in terms of (1) whether the dean's personality (and associated behaviors) matches the phases; and (2) whether the dean's personality (and behaviors) matches the particular subgroup's personality type (and related expectations of decanal behavior). In other words, since the phase dictates the expectations of the actors in an organization (according to Parsons), faculty will anticipate that the dean will act symmetrically with those phase expectations. If deans are mismatched with the phase, having been appointed during another phase, for example, then they may not be able to conform to those expectations, and the faculty may view them with disfavor. Further, if a subgroup of faculty finds itself dispositionally different from the dean regardless of phase, it will also view the dean unfavorably. (The corollary to this, of course, is that some faculty will always be out of synchronization with the phase, though they may be isomorphic with the dean.)

Lacking empirical evidence at this date, it is not possible to determine whether "matched" personalities (deans and faculty subgroup) will always result in higher evaluations, or whether all faculty, regardless of subgroup (subgroups, incidentally, are no doubt linked to traditional disciplines), will rate deans highly if they have personalities appropriate to the phase. To put the discussion into somewhat less abstract terms, it is not clear whether the faculty in the economics department will rate a dean highly only when the latter has an "economics personality," regardless of phase, or whether they will view the dean as effective when dean and phase are matched, regardless of whether the dean is an economist. In sum, views of managerial effectiveness may be a function of matching of phases and deans, or of matching of deans and disciplinary faculty, or of some combination of both. In Figure 9.3 these various possibilities are displayed.

There remains the final merging of these notions of faculty subculture and Parsonian phase with the earlier discussions of different types of organizations in the Pfeffer framework. The question must be asked whether in different kinds of organizations that proceed through different phases, faculty subcultures differ from one another in their evaluations of the dean. For example, does an NT subculture

Figure 9.3
Matching of Dean's Personality, Faculty Subgroup
Personality, and Organizational Phase

| | FACULTY SUBGROUP TYPE I | | FACULTY SUBGROUP TYPE II | |
	Phase I	*Phase II*	*Phase I*	*Phase II*
DEAN TYPE I	Exact Match	Dean Subgroup Match/ Phase Mismatch	Dean Phase Match/ Subgroup Mismatch	Exact Mismatch
DEAN TYPE II	Exact Mismatch	Dean Phase Match/ Subgroup Mismatch	Dean Subgroup Match/ Phase Mismatch	Exact Match

in a political/coalition type organization in a goal-attainment phase differ from an NT subculture in a professional type organization undergoing the same phase? Referring to Figure 9.3, the question is whether different cell entries are required depending on the type of organization being depicted. Again, the answer awaits empirical validation, but it would appear that the dimensions in the Pfeffer typology — goals/means consensus and locus of control — are vital stimuli to the faculty. They will differentially affect faculty subcultures of different types. Sensation-thinking types (STs) will doubtless feel more comfortable in a bureaucratic organization, regardless of phase and regardless of the dean's personality type. Conversely, it would seem reasonable that deans whose personalities do not "fit" the organizational type will be viewed unfavorably by all faculty (but perhaps somewhat less unfavorably by the subcultures that are closer to the deans' personalities). In sum, the "culture" of the organization demands a matched dean.

At the outset of the chapter, it was noted that the managerial effectiveness of the dean might be determined not so much on the basis of actual performance as by ancillary qualities. "Personal effectiveness" resulting from involvement of deans directly with the faculty may not be as important to the "impressions" that faculty receive as are other roles played in the course of satisfying organizational needs of the office of the dean. That is, faculty views of administrator effectiveness in resource allocation, curriculum revision, personnel matters, and fiscal concerns may not be as relevant as the image of deans as they play out various power options. Indeed, it is in the realm of "integration" and "latency" that deans have the greatest impact on the faculty's sense of themselves as autonomous professionals. While the provision of conditions whereby faculty can act as professionals (i.e., in goal-attainment and adaptation phases) may in fact be more crucial in the long-run attainment of ego satisfaction of faculty, there is some reason to believe that in a political environment, faculty will be more attentive to "stroking" (particularly in phases of the organizational life cycle characterized by decline). If this is true, faculty perceptions of decanal effectiveness will be more determined by the deans' activities in areas quite different from those normally associated with "effective" behavior. Decline, for example, as has been noted, typically calls for orientations and modalities of meaning that do not assuage faculty sensitivities.

In the long run, of course, it is useful to consider whether organizations that are "political" in character, as defined in the Pfeffer model, have the potential for being as effective as they might. In such organizations much energy is expended in conflict adjudication. Though some theorists would assert that conflict is functional for organizational adaptation (Deutsch, 1973), others suggest that proper organizational design may mitigate nonfunctional dissipation of energy in political directions. If organizations move toward the professional model, it might be expected that the deans' effectiveness may more properly be associated with substantive organizational and task design, instead of with affective concerns, since a climate of trust and rationality (read "collegiality") would permit faculty to be more task oriented. The activities of deans in this kind of organization might require yet a different personality disposition than would be needed in a political system.

To conclude, it appears that effective administration depends importantly on the type of organization, its phases, the kinds of power used, and the personalities of both administrator and faculty. Understanding the appropriate "fit" among these will lead to more productive leadership and more favorable impressions of that leadership.

Conclusion

Institutional Governance and Individual Responsibility

One of the organizing perspectives in this book is the notion that college and university decision making can be explained using extant theory from the literature on organizational behavior in general. I did not find it necessary to invent a special explanatory framework and terminology on the grounds that higher education is *sui generis*. I agree with Lincoln, Hanada, and Olson (1981) that "organizational arrangements are not random, that they reflect highly patterned social and cultural phenomena to which deterministic explanatory models may be profitably applied." Thus, I have borrowed heavily from a half-dozen or so theories that seem parsimoniously to yield meaningful explanations of the ways in which this "unusual" enterprise works. I certainly do not mean to suggest that higher education is "homologous" with other organizations, as Blau asserts. I do wish to assert, on the other hand, that the "tools of analysis" are homologous.

I have argued that in contrast to some notions in the current literature on the organization of colleges and universities, there are not two distinct decision-making structures — the collegium and the bureaucracy — with decisions falling in one or the other or, often ambiguously, in both. Nor are there two structures on a continuum. Rather, I have suggested that only one decision-making structure exists, with different parts employed as the contingencies of organizational decision making demand. These different parts are not mysterious and unique to higher education, but are responses to pressures existing in all kinds of organizations. Moreover, the forms of organization that are found in higher education are not significantly different from those in other organizations of similar complexity and goal types.

Which part of the structure is utilized is subject to a number of influences, some of which can be explained as rational adaptations to organizational needs stemming from environment and technology. These have direct impacts on the organization's requirements for information up and down the hierarchy and for coordination of its separated line suborganizations.

Some of the influences result from the exercise of politics. Whether an institution is or is not political depends on the degree of goal consensus and control by authorities, which are, in turn, partially influenced by the culture of collegiality. The modern university, especially in the late 1980s, is subject to a number of stresses that make traditional bureaucratic hierarchies inadequate to the complex prerequisites that must be met by successful organizations. Rapid shifts in the environment (reduced numbers of students, threats of lesser support from federal, state, and eleemosynary sources), extremely autonomous line units, and a multi-tiered decision-making structure that is not able to communicate quickly and accurately all combine to force the institution to create forms of organization that augment a simple hierarchy. The result is the familiar university decision framework—for example, the senates and committee structures—now commonly distributed throughout higher education.

In addition to the information-processing explanation of governance, I suggested above that interdependence among transformation units in the college or university creates needs for coordination and control and that such control allegedly cannot be accomplished through bureaucratic modes. The technology of the tasks, I would claim, suggests the need for a mode of coordination that is not programmable in the March and Simon (1958) sense. The alternatives, as offered by Van de Ven, Delbecq, and Koenig (1976), are coordination by personal means and through groups, with the latter most frequently following from increases in uncertainties of tasks and from greater reciprocal interdependence among task groups. Governance, in other words, is a structural accommodation to purported interdependencies among transformation units and to uncertainties about the processes of transformation, where connections between units cannot be made through appeal to superordinates, as in a bureaucracy. More precisely, the chain of command cannot help adjudicate differences among academic departments as they seek to work through curricular overlaps. It must be done, according to this theory, through group coordination methods. We have given those methods a unique label, governance, but it is instead a rather typical industrial coordinating rose by another name.

Thus, the mystique of "governance" as a form of decision making that meets the allegedly unique needs of the profession of higher education can be somewhat dissipated by explaining the structures of governance in social science terms — namely, as responses to organizational needs for better information flow and better coordination.

But there still remains some unexplained variance in the forms and operations of different governance structures. How can we account for the alternative forms of governance in colleges and universities that seem to favor certain units — academic or nonacademic — over others? How also can we account for the dispersion of authority across the various possible decision makers in higher education — that is, across such decision units as individual faculty member, individual administrator, two-person structures, and multiple decision structures? Here the explanation lies in the organizational literature on "power" and on "collegiality" — antithetical pulls in every organization. On the one hand, coalitions of individuals and groups conspire (not necessarily in a negative sense) to obtain and sustain power that benefits them in particular. On the other, individuals and groups renounce power in favor of trust and rationality.

I have suggested that those units (academic or nonacademic) that occupy key organizational positions with respect to either improved information flow or better coordination and control (i.e., the Galbraith and/or Van de Ven, Delbecq, & Koenig explanations) will be seen to be in positions not only to benefit themselves but to influence the very design of the governance structure to enhance both their benefits and their power. Whether this is functional — both for the organization and for the persons — depends on several factors. If powerful departments and their members accrue benefits to themselves by virtue of their talents and achievements, then it may be functional for the organization in the short run continue to "feed" that power. On the other hand, if the power is gained through subversive means without due concern for others, neither the organization nor the individuals will succeed in the long run. It would seem that collegial modes of operation, which are after all most consonant with "organizational development" values, might better suit the team building and individual growth objectives of successful organizations. Short-run, market-driven interactions, however adaptive, will, as Ouchi notes, destroy the clan. I have clearly adopted a "functionalist" perspective in this book, despite the many critics of this approach. The longevity of institutions of higher learning in this country may attest to the truth of the principle of "equifinality." Many structural approaches to attending to the functional prerequisites have served to sustain different kinds of institutions.

Of course, mere longevity does not necessarily connote effectiveness or efficiency—a question I began to address in Part 2 of this book. There I examined the relationships of various structural characteristics of universities as they may affect the perceptions of faculty members. I was concerned with the identification of structures in the university that are accountable for performing different functions, particularly as the institution moves through cycles of stress and success. Recognition of the shifts in responsibility and the perceptions of effectiveness by constituents of the university helps to clarify why the decision-making structures that have evolved over the years are criticized or praised.

James Thompson (1967) has suggested that efficiency is enhanced when workers and/or tasks that are interdependent are organized together in substructures, thus minimizing costs of coordination. In higher education, we follow this maxim by creating departments comprising faculty teaching related subjects. In point of fact, however, the gain in efficiency is at a cost of effectiveness. Knowledge as a criterion of task clustering ignores the larger questions of cross-disciplinary connections of subject matters for liberal education and student growth and development. I have pointed out (here and in other writings) that discipline-based departmentalization is a product of the addition of the research function to the university task agenda. Research efficiencies are, for the most part, enhanced by grouping by discipline. The explanation of decision-making structures in higher education must be understood in terms of the dominance of research and the power of coalitions engaged in research. Vertical and lateral communication needs under a different priority structure with different groupings of faculty might be quite different and might call for decision-making bodies with strikingly different dimensions from those we find today.

Governance by Committee

The allocation of decision making to *ad hoc* committees in higher education is common. I have suggested above that such decision-making bodies serve well the vertical and horizontal information flow needs of the system by bringing together experts with knowledge of the issues at hand. I also noted, however, that this mechanism violates the nearly sacrosanct homily that "authority and responsibility should not be separated." Because committees serve middle-management functions, they perform controlling functions. But governance by committees has two latent functions (perhaps dysfunctions). First, responsibility is not fixed in any one person or group of persons, with negative sanctions for poor performance. If a curriculum committee makes a poor decision, it will not be held accountable as a whole, nor will any one of its members be "called to task." Second, committee decisions reduce the visibility of uncomfortable asymmetries of power, which might exist in a one-on-one relationship (cf. March & Simon, 1958). A negative tenure decision or a rejection of a budget or curriculum change request is more acceptable to lower participants when it comes from a group, instead of one person. Groups tend to dampen interpersonal prejudices and biases, though they may promote group bias.

Thus, academia, thought to be *sui generis* as an organizational phenomenon, can be seen as quite similar to nonacademic organizations in terms of its structural adaptations, its use of power, and the dispersion of authority over various classes of decisions. With increased clarity as to the sources of influence on decision making in higher education, we can look with greater understanding to the ways in which the educational missions of our colleges and universities can better be accomplished.

A Concluding Note

Corporate cultures and formal structures are needed to maintain order in organizational life. Both can be manipulated toward varying ends. They can orient behavior, control it, or free it. A long history of organizational theory argues for an integration of (or at least a balance between) the needs of the organization for control of workers to achieve organizational aims with the needs of individuals for freedom and self-determination. In different kinds of organizations, there are varying personal needs for freedom and varying degrees of tolerance for uncertainty, both on the organization and the individual side. Some organizations are most effective under loosely coupled conditions, while others thrive under more tightly controlled arrangements. Some individuals need considerable discretionary power, while others prefer directions. In the best organizations, there is a match between the two. At issue is whether that match also serves the clients of the organization. More particular to questions raised in this book, are the structure for decision making in higher education and the predispositions of its decision makers suited to the systems they serve — society and their personal needs? Or is the match an unfortunate product of historical circumstance, which maintains itself in some sort of neurotic condition, ill-suited to the growth of society and of higher education?

In this book, I have attempted to explicate the complexities of the decision-making structure in higher education. My purpose has been to explain the reasons why the current structure exists. It now remains to determine whether that structure serves the functions that it ought.

REFERENCES

Abdel-Halim, Ahmed A. "Personality and Task Moderators of Subordinate Responses to Perceived Leader Behavior." *Human Relations*, January 1981, *34*, 1, 73–88.

Aldrich, Howard E. & Jeffrey Pfeffer. "Environments of Organizations." *Annual Review of Sociology*, 1976, *2*, 79–105.

Allen, Robert W., Dan L. Madison, Lyman Porter, Patricia Renwick, & Bronston T. Mays. "Organizational Politics: Tactics and Characteristics of Its Actors." *California Management Review*, Fall 1979, *32*, 1, 77–83.

Argyris, Chris & Donald A. Schon. *Theory in Practice.* San Francisco: Jossey-Bass Publishers, 1974.

Astin, Alexander W. & Rita A. Scherrei. *Maximizing Leadership Effectiveness.* San Francisco: Jossey-Bass Publishers, 1980.

Astley, W. Graham & Paramjit S. Sachdeva. "Structural Sources of Intraorganizational Power: A Theoretical Snythesis." *Academy of Management Review*, January 1984, *9*, 1, 104–113.

Bacharach, Samuel B. & Edward E. Lawler. *Power and Politics in Organizations.* San Francisco: Jossey-Bass Publishers, 1980.

Bachman, Jerald G. "Faculty Satisfaction and the Dean's Influence: An Organizational Study of Twelve Liberal Arts Colleges." *Journal of Applied Psychology*, 1968, *52*, 1, 55–61.

Baldridge, J. Victor. *Power and Conflict in the University.* New York: John Wiley & Sons, 1971.

Baldridge, J. Victor, David V. Curtis, George Ecker, & Gary L. Riley. *Policy Making and Effective Leadership.* San Francisco: Jossey-Bass Publishers, 1978.

Barnard, Chester I. *The Functions of the Executive.* Cambridge, MA: Harvard University Press, 1938.

Becher, Tony. "Principles and Politics: An Interpretive Framework for University Management." *International Journal of Institutional Management in Higher Education*, November 1984, *8*, 3, 191–199.

Becher, Tony & M. Kogan. *Process and Structure in Higher Education.* London: Heinemann Educational Books, Inc., 1980.

Becker, Selwyn W. & Gerald Gordon. "People, Personality and Complex Organizations." *Journal of the College and University Personnel Association*, 1964, *16*, 17–23.

Becker, Selwyn W. & Gerald Gordon. "An Entrepreneurial Theory of Organization, Part I: Patterns of Formal Organizations." *Administrative Science Quarterly*, December 1966, *11*, 3, 315–344.

Beer, Michael. "A Social Systems Model for Organizational Development," in Thomas G. Cummings (ed.), *Systems Theory for Organizational Development.* Chichester, England: John Wiley & Sons, 1980, 73–114.

Bendor, Jonathon B. *Parallel Systems, Redundancy in Government.* Berkeley: University of California Press, 1985.

Berger, Peter L. & Luckmann, Thomas. *The Social Construction of Reality*. New York: Doubleday, 1966.

Bergquist, William N. & Steven R. Phillips. *A Handbook for Faculty Development*. Washington, DC: Council for the Advancement of Small Colleges, 1975.

Berlo, David K. *The Process of Communication*. New York: Holt, Rinehart & Winston, 1960.

Bess, James L. "The Medium and the Educational Message, A 'McLuhanistic' Look at Philosophy and Practice in Higher Education, 1825–1835 and 1875–1885." Unpublished manuscript, 1967.

Bess, James L. "Patterns of Satisfactions of Organizational Prerequisites and Personal Needs in University Departments of High and Low Quality." Unpublished Ph.D. Dissertation, University of California, Berkeley, 1971.

Bess, James L. "Integrating Student and Faculty Life Cycles." *Review of Educational Research*, Fall 1973a, *43*, 4, 377–403.

Bess, James L. "Patterns of Satisfactions of Organizational Prerequisites and Personal Needs in University Academic Departments." *Sociology of Education*, Winter 1973b, *46*, 1, 99–114.

Bess, James L. Review of *The Organization of Academic Work*, by Peter M. Blau. *Journal of Higher Education*, October 1974, *55*, 7.

Bess, James L. "The Motivation to Teach." *Journal of Higher Education*, May/June 1977, *48*, 1, 243–258.

Bess, James L. "Anticipatory Socialization of Graduate Students." *Research in Higher Education*, 1978, *8*, 4, 289–317.

Bess, James L. "Classroom and Management Decision Using Student Data." *Journal of Higher Education*, May/June 1979, *50*, 1, 256–279.

Bess, James L. "The Social Psychology of Commitment to Teaching." Unpublished manuscript, New York University, 1981.

Bess, James L. *University Organization: A Matrix Analysis of the Academic Professions*. New York: Human Sciences Press, 1982.

Beyer, Janice M. "Ideologies, Values, and Decision Making in Organizations," in Paul C. Nystrom & William H. Starbuck (eds.), *Handbook of Organizational Design*, Volume 2. New York: Oxford University Press, 1981, 166–202.

Beyer, Janice M. "Power Dependencies and the Distribution of Influence in Universities." *Research in the Sociology of Organizations*, 1982, *1*, 167–208.

Beyer, Janice M. & Thomas M. Lodahl. "A Comparative Study of Patterns of Influence in the United States and English Universities." *Administrative Science Quarterly*, 1976, *21*, 104–129.

Bidwell, Charles E. "The Administrative Role and Satisfaction in Teaching." *The Journal of Educational Sociology*, September 1955, *29*, 1, 41–46.

Biglan, Anthony. "The Characteristics of Subject Matter in Different Academic Areas." *Journal of Applied Psychology*, 1973, *57*, 195–203.

Blackburn, Robert T. & Robert J. Havighurst. "Career Patterns of Distinguished Male Social Scientists." Paper presented at the annual meeting of the American Educational Research Association, San Francisco, April 1979.

Blau, Peter M. *Exchange and Power in Social Life*. New York: John Wiley & Sons, 1964.

Blau, Peter M. *The Organization of Academic Work*. New York: John Wiley & Sons, 1973.

Blau, Peter M. & Richard A. Schoenherr. *The Structure of Organizations*. New York: Basic Books, Inc., 1971.

Bloland, Harland G. "Toward a Phenomenological Politics of Higher Education Decision Making." Paper presented at the annual meeting of the American Educational Research Association, Los Angeles, April 1981.

Blood, Milton R. "Organizational Control of Performance Through Self-Rewarding," in Burt King, Siegfried Streufert, & Fred E. Fielder (eds.), *Managerial Control and Organizational Democracy*. Washington, DC: V. H. Winston & Sons, 1978.

Bloom, Benjamin S. (ed.). *Taxonomy of Educational Objectives*. New York: David McKay Co., Inc., 1956.

Bohannan, Paul. "The *Ad Hoc* Community." *The Center Magazine*, May/June 1980, 36–37.

Bowen, Howard R. *Academic Compensation*. New York: Teachers Insurance and Annuity Association, 1978.

Bragg, Ann Kiffer. "The Socialization of Academic Department Heads: Past Patterns and Future Possibilities." Paper presented at the annual meeting of the Association for the Study of Higher Education, Washington, DC, 1981.

Bresser, Rudi K. "The Context of University Departments: Differences Between Fields of Higher and Lower Levels of Paradigm Development." *Research in Higher Education*, 1984, *20*, 1, 3–15.

Brooks, William D. & Phillip Emmert. *Interpersonal Communication*. Dubuque, IA: William C. Brown Co., Publishers, 1976.

Brown, Martha A. "What Kind of Leaders Do Faculty Members Want?" *College Management*, January 1973, *8*, 1, 25–27.

Bucher, Rue & Joan Stelling. "Four Characteristics of Professional Organizations." *Journal of Health and Social Behavior*, March 1969, *10*, 3–15.

Calder, Bobby J. "An Attribution Theory of Leadership," in Barry M. Staw & Gerald R. Salancik (eds.), *New Directions in Organizational Behavior*. Chicago: St. Clair Press, 1977.

Cameron, Kim S. "Measuring Organizational Effectiveness in Institutions of Higher Education." *Administrative Science Quarterly*, 1978, *23*, 604–632.

Cameron, Kim S. "Dimensions of Organizational Effectiveness in Colleges and Universities." *Academy of Management Journal*, March 1981, *24*, 25–47.

Cameron, Kim S. "A Study of Organizational Effectiveness and Its Predictors." *Management Science*, January 1986a, *32*, 5, 86–112.

Cameron, Kim S. "Effectiveness as Paradox." *Management Science*, May 1986b, *32*, 5, 539–553.

Cameron, Kim S. & David S. Whetten. "Perceptions of Organizational Effectiveness Over Organizational Life Cycles." *Administrative Science Quarterly*, December 1981, *26*, 4, 525–544.

Cameron, Kim S. & David S. Whetten. *Organizational Effectiveness, A Comparison of Multiple Models*. New York: Academic Press, 1983.

Cameron, Kim S. & David S. Whetten. "Models of the Organizational Life Cycle: Applications to Higher Education," in James L. Bess (ed.), *College and University Organization*. New York: New York University Press, 1984.

Campbell, John P. & Robert D. Pritchard. "Motivation Theory in Industrial and Organizational Psychology," in Marvin D. Dunnette (ed.), *Handbook of Industrial and Organizational Psychology*. Chicago: Rand McNally, 1976, 63–130.

Cares, Robert C. & Robert T. Blackburn. "Faculty Self-Actualization: Factors Affecting Career Success." *Research in Higher Education*, October 1978, *9*, 2, 123–136.

Carnegie Foundation for the Advancement of Teaching. *The Control of the Campus.* Washington, DC: Author, 1982.

Carrell, M. R. & J. E. Dittrich. "Equity Theory: The Recent Literature, Methodological Considerations, and New Directions." *Academy of Management Review,* April 1978, *3*, 2, 202–208.

Carzo, Rocco, Jr. & John N. Yanouzas. *Formal Organizations: A Systems Approach.* Homewood, IL: Richard D. Irwin, Inc., 1967.

Catania, A. Charles. "Eliciting Reinforcement, and Stimulus Control," in Robert Glaser (ed.), *The Nature of Reinforcement.* New York: Academic Press, 1971.

Centers, Richard & Daphne E. Bugental. "Intrinsic and Extrinsic Job Motivators Among Different Segments of the Working Population." *Journal of Applied Psychology,* June 1966, *50*, 3, 193–197.

Centra, John A. "The Effectiveness of Student Feedback in Modifying College Instruction." *Journal of Educational Psychology,* December 1973, *65*, 3, 395–401.

Centra, John A. *Faculty Development Practices in U.S. Colleges and Universities.* Princeton, NJ: Educational Testing Service, 1976.

Centra, John A. "The How and Why of Evaluating Teaching." *New Directions for Higher Education,* Spring 1977, *5*, 1, 93–106.

Chaffee, Ellen E. "The Role of Rationality in University Budgeting." *Research in Higher Education,* 1983a, *14*, 4, 387–406.

Chaffee, Ellen E. *Rational Decisionmaking in Higher Education.* Boulder, CO: National Center for Higher Education Management Systems, 1983b.

Chandler, A. D. *The Visible Hand: The Managerial Revolution in American Business.* Cambridge, MA: The Belknap Press, 1977.

Charns, Martin P., Paul R. Lawrence, & Marvin R. Weisbord. "Organizing Multiple-Function Professionals in Academic Medical Centers," in Paul C. Nystrom & William H. Starbuck (eds.), *Prescriptive Models of Organizations.* New York: Elsevier Science Publishing Co., Inc., TIMS Studies in the Management Sciences, 1977, *5*, 71–88.

Chell, Elizabeth. *Participation and Organization: A Social Psychological Approach.* New York: Schocken Books, 1985.

Child, John. "Strategies of Control and Organizational Behavior." *Administrative Science Quarterly,* 1973, *18*, 1–17.

Childers, Marie E. "What Is Political About Bureaucratic-Collegial Decision-Making?" *The Review of Higher Education,* Fall 1981, *5*, 1, 25–47.

Clark, Burton R. "The Organizational Saga in Higher Education." *Administrative Science Quarterly,* June 1972, *17*, 2, 178–184.

Clark, Burton R. "The Many Pathways of Academic Coordination." *Higher Education,* May 1979, *8*, 3, 251–267.

Clark, Burton R. *The Higher Educational System.* Berkeley: University of California Press, 1983.

Clark, Terry N. "The Concept of Power: Some Overemployed and Underrecognized Dimensions—An Examination with Special Reference to the Local Community." (Southwestern) *Social Science Quarterly,* December 1967, 271–286.

Clay, Rex J. "A Validation Study of Maslow's Hierarchy of Needs Theory." *Research in Education,* July 1977. (ERIC Document Reproduction Service No. ED 150 416)

Cobb, Anthony T. "An Episodic Model of Power: Toward an Integration of Theory and Research." *Academy of Management Review,* July 1984, *9*, 3, 482–493.

Cohen, Michael D. & James G. March. *Leadership and Ambiguity.* New York: McGraw Hill, 1974.

Coltrin, Sally & William F. Glueck. "The Effect of Leadership Roles on the Satisfaction and Productivity of University Research Professors." *Academy of Management Journal*, March 1977, *20*, 1, 101–116.

Cope, Robert G. "Bases of Power, Administrative Preferences and Job Satisfaction: A Structural Approach." *Journal of Vocational Behavior*, October 1972, *2*, 4, 457–466.

Cope, Robert G. "Bases of Power, Administrative Preferences and Job Satisfaction: A Situational Approach." *Journal of Vocational Behavior*, January 1973, *3*, 1, 1–9.

Cotton, Chester C. "Measurement of Power-Balancing Styles and Some of Their Correlates." *Administrative Science Quarterly*, June 1976, *21*, 2, 307–319.

Crozier, Michel. *The Bureaucratic Phenomenon*. Chicago: University of Chicago Press, 1964.

Crozier, Michel & Erhard Friedberg. "The Limits of a Theory of Structural Contingency," in Michel Crozier & Erhard Friedberg (eds.), *Actors and Systems, The Politics of Collective Action* (Arthur Goldhammer, trans.). Chicago: University of Chicago Press, 1980.

Cullen, John B. *The Structure of Professionalism*. Princeton, NJ: Petrocelli Books, 1979.

Cummings, L. L., Michael J. O'Connell, & George P. Huber. "Informational and Structural Determinants of Decision-Maker Satisfaction," in Bert King, Siegfried Streutert, & Fred E. Fiedler (eds.), *Managerial Control and Organizational Democracy*. Washington, DC: V. H. Winston & Sons, 1978, 231–246.

Cyert, Richard & James G. March. *A Behavioral Theory of the Firm*. Englewood Cliffs, NJ: Prentice-Hall, 1963.

Daft, Richard L. & Robert H. Lengel. "Information Richness: A New Approach to Managerial Behavior and Organizational Design." *Research in Organizational Behavior*, 1984, *6*, 191–233.

Daft, Richard L. & Norman B. Macintosh. "A Tentative Exploration Into the Amount and Equivocality of Information Processing in Organizational Work Units." *Administrative Science Quarterly*, June 1981, *26*, 2, 207–244.

Dahl, Robert. "The Concept of Power." *Behavioral Science*, July 1957, *2*, 201–215.

Day, Robert & JoAnne V. Day. "A Review of the Current State of Negotiated Order Theory: An Appreciation and a Critique." *Sociological Quarterly*, Winter 1977, *18*, 1, 126–140.

Deal, Terrence E. & Allan A. Kennedy. *Corporate Cultures: The Rites and Rituals of Corporate Life*. Reading, MA: Addison-Wesley, 1982.

DeCharms, Richard. *Personal Causation*. New York: Academic Press, 1968.

Deutsch, Morton. *The Resolution of Conflict*. New Haven: Yale University Press, 1973.

DeVries, David L. "The Relationship of Role Expectations to Faculty Behavior." *Research in Higher Education*, 1975, *3*, 2, 111–129.

Dewey, John. *Democracy and Education*. New York: The Macmillan Company, 1916.

Dewey, John. *Human Nature and Conduct*. New York: Holt, Rinehart & Winston, 1922.

Dewey, John. *Art as Experience*. New York: G. P. Putnam's Sons, 1934.

Diesing, Paul. *Reason in Society; Five Types of Decisions and Their Social Conditions*. Westport, CT: Greenwood Press, 1962.

Dill, David D. "The Management of Academic Culture: Notes on the Management of Meaning and Social Integration." *Higher Education*, 1982, *11*, 303–320.

Dornbusch, Sanford M. "Perspectives from Sociology: Organizational Evaluation of Faculty Performances," in Darrell R. Lewis and William E. Becker, Jr. (eds.), *Academic Rewards in Higher Education*. Cambridge, MA: Ballinger Publishing Company, 1979, 41–60.

Driver, Michael. "Decision Style and Organizational Behavior: Implications for

Academia," in J. L. Bess (ed.), *College and University Organization*. New York: New York University Press, 1984.

Durkheim, Emile. *The Division of Labor in Society* (George Simpson, trans.). New York: Macmillan, 1933.

Eastcott, Leslie R. "Understanding Decision-Making in a University Faculty." *The Journal of Educational Administration*, October 1977, *15*, 2, 290–309.

Etzioni, Amitai. "Authority Structure and Organizational Effectiveness." *Administrative Science Quarterly*, June 1959, *4*, 1, 43–67.

Etzioni, Amitai. *A Comparative Analysis of Complex Organizations*. New York: The Free Press, 1961.

Etzioni, Amitai. *Modern Organizations*. Englewood Cliffs, NJ: Prentice-Hall, 1964.

Falbo, T. "Multidimensional Scaling of Power Strategies." *Journal of Personality and Social Psychology*, August 1977, *35*, 8, 537–547.

Fiedler, Fred E. *A Theory of Leadership Effectiveness*. New York: McGraw-Hill, 1967.

Filley, Alan & R. J. Aldag. "Organizational Growth and Types: Lessons from Small Institutions," in Barry M. Staw & Larry L. Cummings (eds.), *Research in Organizational Behavior*, Volume 2. Greenwich, CT: JAI Press, 1980, 45–80.

Filley, Alan & Robert J. House. *Managerial Process and Organizational Behavior*. Glenview, IL: Scott, Foresman, 1969.

Finkelstein, Martin J. "Three Decades of Research on American Academics." Unpublished Ph.D. Dissertation, State University of New York at Buffalo, 1978.

Finkelstein, Martin J. "The Dimensions of Colleagueship Among College and University Faculty." Paper presented at the annual meeting of the American Educational Research Association, Los Angeles, April 1981. (ERIC Document Reproduction Service No. ED 201 275)

Finkelstein, Martin J. *The American Academic Profession*. Columbus: Ohio State University Press, 1984.

Fisher, Cynthia D. "The Effects of Personal Control, Competence, and Extrinsic Reward Systems on Intrinsic Motivation." *Organizational Behavior and Human Performance*, June 1978, *21*, 3, 273–287.

Flanagan, John C. "The Critical Incident Technique." *Psychological Bulletin*, July 1954, *51*, 4, 327–358.

Francis, Arthur, Jeremy Turk, & Paul W. Willman (eds.). *Power, Efficiency and the Institution*. London: Heinemann Educational Books, Inc., 1983.

Frank, Andrew G. "Administrative Role Definitions and Social Change." *Human Organization*, Winter 1963, *22*, 238–242.

Frederickson, James W. "The Effect of Structure on Strategic Decision Process," in John A. Pearce II & Richard B. Robinson, Jr. (eds.), *Academy of Management Proceedings*. Columbia, SC: Darby Press, 1984, 12–21.

French, John R. P., Jr. & B. H. Raven. "The Bases of Social Power," in D. Cartwright (ed.), *Studies in Social Power*. Ann Arbor: University of Michigan Press, 1959, 150–167.

French, John R. P., Jr., C. John Tupper, & Ernst F. Mueller. *Work Load of University Professors*. Institute for Social Research Cooperative Research Project No. 2171, The University of Michigan, Ann Arbor, 1965.

Frost, Peter J., Larry F. Moore, Meryl Reis Louis, Craig C. Lundberg, & Joanne Martin (eds.). *Organizational Culture*. Beverly Hills: Sage Publications, Inc., 1985.

Gage, N. L. (ed.). *The Scientific Basis of the Art of Teaching*. New York: Teachers College Press, 1978.

Galbraith, Jay R. *Designing Complex Organizations*. Reading, MA: Addison-Wesley Publishing Company, 1973.

Galbraith, Jay R. *Organization Design*. Reading, MA: Addison-Wesley, 1977.

Gamson, William A. *Power and Discontent*. Homewood, IL: The Dorsey Press, 1968.

Georiou, P. "Goal Paradigm and Notes Toward a Counter Paradigm." *Administrative Science Quarterly*, March 1973, *18*, 3, 291–310.

Gerth, H. H. & C. Wright Mills. *From Max Weber: Essays in Sociology*. New York: Oxford University Press, 1946.

Getzels, Jacob W., James M. Lipham, & Roald F. Campbell. *Educational Administration as a Social Process*. New York: Harper & Row Publishers, 1968.

Ghorpade, Jaisingh (ed.). *Assessment of Organizational Effectiveness*. San Francisco: Jossey-Bass Publishers, 1977.

Glenny, Lyman A. "The Anonymous Leaders of Higher Education." *Journal of Higher Education*, January 1972, *43*, 1, 9–22.

Goodenough, Ward H. *Description and Comparison in Cultural Anthropology*. Chicago: Aldine Publishing Company, 1970.

Goodman, Paul S., Johannes M. Pennings, & Associates. *New Perspectives on Organizational Effectiveness*. San Francisco: Jossey-Bass Publishers, 1977.

Goodwin, Leonard. "The Academic World and the Business World: A Comparison of Occupational Goals." *Sociology of Education*, Spring 1969a, *42*, 2, 170–187.

Goodwin, Leonard. "Occupational Goals and Satisfactions of the American Work Force." *Personnel Psychology*, Autumn 1969b, *22*, 3, 313–325.

Gouldner, Alvin W. *Patterns of Industrial Bureaucracy*. Glencoe, IL: The Free Press, 1954.

Gouldner, Alvin W. "Cosmopolitans and Locals: Toward an Analysis of Latent Social Roles — I." *Administrative Science Quarterly*, December 1957, *1*, 3, 281–306.

Gouldner, Alvin W. "Cosmopolitans and Locals: Toward an Analysis of Latent Social Roles — II." *Administrative Science Quarterly*, March 1958, *2*, 4, 444–480.

Gouldner, Alvin W. "The Norm of Reciprocity." *American Sociological Review*, April 1960, *25*, 2, 161–179.

Grant, Gerald & David Riesman. *The Perpetual Dream*. Chicago: University of Chicago Press, 1978.

Greene, Charles. "The Satisfaction Performance Controversy." *Business Horizons*, 1972, *15*, 5, 31–42.

Gunne, Manny G. & Kenneth P. Mortimer. *Distributions of Authority and Patterns of Governance*. University Park, PA: Center for the Study of Higher Education, Pennsylvania State University, 1975.

Gutek, B. D. "Satisfaction Guaranteed — What Does It Mean?" *Social Policy*, September/October 1978, *9*, 2, 56–60.

Hackman, J. Richard & Greg R. Oldham. "Motivation Through the Design of Work: Test of a Theory." Technical Report No. 6, Department of Administrative Sciences, Yale University, December 1974a.

Hackman, J. Richard & Greg R. Oldham. "The Job Diagnostic Survey: An Instrument for the Diagnosis of Jobs and Evaluation of Job Redesign Projects." Technical Report No. 4, Department of Administrative Sciences, Yale University, May 1974b.

Hackman, J. Richard & Greg R. Oldham. *Work Redesign*. Reading, MA: Addison-Wesley, 1980.

Hall, Douglas T. & Cynthia V. Fukami. "Organizational Design and Adult Learning." *Research in Organizational Behavior*, 1979, *1*, 125–167.

Hamner, W. Clay. "Reinforcement Theory and Contingency Management in Organizational Settings," in Henry L. Tosi & W. Clay Hamner (eds.), *Organizational Behavior and Management: A Contingency Approach*. Chicago: St. Clair Press, 1974, 191–208.

Hanswer, Lawrence M. & Paul M. Muchinsky. "Work as an Information Environment." *Organizational Behavior and Human Performance*, February 1978, *21*, 1, 47–60.

Hardin, Garrett. "The Tragedy of the Commons." *Science*, 1968, *162*, 1243–1248.

Hardy, Cynthia, Ann Langley, Henry Mintzberg, & Janet Rose. "Strategy Formation in the University Setting," in James L. Bess (ed.), *College and University Organization: Insights from the Behavioral Sciences*. New York: New York University Press, 1984, 169–210.

Harrison, P. "Understanding Your Organization's Character." *Harvard Business Review*, May–June 1972, *50*, 3, 119–129.

Helsabeck, Robert E. *The Compound System*. Berkeley: Center for Research and Development in Higher Education, 1973.

Herzberg, Frederick. *Work and the Nature of Man*. Cleveland: World Publishing, 1966.

Herzberg, Frederick, Bernard Mausner, & Barbara Bloch Snyderman. *The Motivation to Work*. New York: John Wiley & Sons, 1959.

Hickson, D. J., C. R. Hinings, C. A. Lee, R. E. Schneck, & J. M. Pennings. "A Strategic Contingencies Theory of Interorganizational Power." *Administrative Science Quarterly*, June 1971, *16*, 2, 216–229.

Hill, Winston W. & Wendell L. French. "Perceptions of Power of Department Chairmen by Professors." *Administrative Science Quarterly*, March 1967, *2*, 4, 548–574.

Hills, F. S. & T. A. Mahoney. "University Budgets and Organizational Decision-Making." *Administrative Science Quarterly*, March 1978, *23*, 3, 454–465.

Hills, R. Jean. *Toward a Science of Organization*. Eugene, OR: Center for the Advanced Study of Educational Administration, University of Oregon, 1968.

Hind, R. R., Sanford M. Dornbusch, & W. Richard Scott. "A Theory of Evaluation Applied to a University Faculty." *Sociology of Education*, Winter 1974, *47*, 1, 114–128.

Hinings, C. R., D. J. Hickson, J. M. Pennings, & R. E. Schneck. "Structural Conditions of Intraorganizational Power." *Administrative Science Quarterly*, March 1974, *19*, 1, 22–44.

Hodgkinson, Harold L. "Adult Development: Implications for Faculty and Administrators." *Educational Record*, Fall 1974, *55*, 4, 263–274.

Homans, George C. *The Human Group*. New York: Harcourt, Brace & World, 1950.

House, Robert J. "A Path-Goal Theory of Leader Effectiveness." *Administrative Science Quarterly*, September 1971, *16*, 3, 321–338.

Hoy, Wayne K. & William J. Kupersmith. "The Concept of Trust: An Empirical Assessment." Paper presented at the annual meeting of the American Educational Research Association, New Orleans, 1984.

Hoy, Wayne K. & Cecil G. Miskel. *Educational Administration*. New York: Random House, 1982.

Hrebiniak, Lawrence G. *Complex Organizations*. St. Paul: West Publishing Company, 1978.

Jacobson, Eugene, W. W. Charters, Jr., & S. Lieberman. "The Use of the Role Concept in the Study of Complex Organizations." *Journal of Social Issues*, 1951, *7*, 3, 18–27.

Kanter, Rosabeth Moss. "Commitment and Social Organization: A Study of Commitment Mechanisms in Utopian Communities." *American Sociological Review*, August 1968, *33*, 4, 499–517.

Kanter, Rosabeth Moss. "Power Failure in Management Circuits." *Harvard Business Review*, July/August 1979, 65–75.

Katz, Daniel & Robert L. Kahn. *The Social Psychology of Organizations*, 2nd Ed. New York: John Wiley & Sons, 1978.

Katz, Ralph & John Van Maanen. "The Loci of Work Satisfaction: Job, Interaction, and Policy." *Human Relations*, May 1977, *30*, 5, 469–486.

Katzell, Raymond A. & Daniel Yankelovich. *Work Productivity and Job Satisfaction*. New York: Harcourt Brace Jovanovich, 1975.

Keeley, Michael. "Impartiality and Participant-Interest Theories of Organizational Effectiveness." *Administrative Science Quarterly*, March 1984, *29*, 1, 1–25.

Kelly, Richard & Darrell Hart. "The Role Preferences of Faculty in Different Age Groups and Academic Disciplines." *Sociology of Education*, Summer 1971, *44*, 3, 351–357.

Kenen, Peter B. & Regina H. Kenen. "Who Thinks Who's in Charge Here: Faculty Perceptions of Influence and Power in the University." *Sociology of Education*, April 1978, *51*, 113–123.

Kerr, Clark. *The Uses of the University*. Cambridge, MA: Harvard University Press, 1963.

Kerr, Steven. "Substitutes for Leadership: Some Explications for Organizational Design." *Organization and Administrative Sciences*, 1977, *8*, 1, 135–146.

Kerr, Steven & John M. Jermier. "Substitutes for Leadership: Their Meaning and Measurement." *Organizational Behavior and Human Performance*, 1978, *22*, 375–403.

Khandwalla, P. *The Design of Organizations*. New York: Harcourt Brace Jovanovich, 1977.

Kilmann, Ralph H. *Social System Design: Normative Theory and the MAPS Design Technology*. New York: Elsevier North-Holland, 1977.

Kilmann, Ralph H. & Richard P. Herden. "Towards a Systematic Methodology for Evaluating the Impact of Interventions on Organizational Effectiveness." *Academy of Management Review*, July 1976, *1*, 3, 87–98.

Kimberly, John R., Robert H. Miles, & Associates. *The Organizational Life Cycle*. San Francisco: Jossey-Bass Publishers, 1980.

Kipnis, D., S. M. Schmidt, & I. Wilkinson. "Intraorganizational Influence Tactics — Explorations in Getting One's Way." *Journal of Applied Psychology*, 1980, *65*, 4, 440–452.

Kochen, Manfred & Karl W. Deutsch. *Decentralization*. Cambridge, MA: Oelgeschlager, Gunn and Hain, Publishers, Inc., 1980.

Kohlberg, Lawrence. "Stage and Sequence: The Cognitive-Developmental Approach to Socialization," in D. Goslin (ed.), *Handbook of Socialization Theory and Research*. Chicago: Rand McNally, 1969, 347–480.

Kotter, J. P. *Organizational Dynamics: Diagnosis and Intervention*. Reading, MA: Addison-Wesley, 1978.

Krathwohl, David R., Benjamin S. Bloom, & Bertram B. Massia. *Taxonomy of Educational Objectives*. New York: David McKay Co., Inc., 1964.

Krause, M. S. "Use of Social Situations for Research Purposes." *American Psychologist*, August 1970, *25*, 8, 748–752.

Ladd, Everett C. & Seymour M. Lipset. *The Divided Academy*. New York: McGraw Hill, 1975.

Lawler, Edward E., III. *Motivation in Work Organizations*. Monterey, CA: Brooks/Cole Publishing Company, 1973.

Lawler, Edward E., III. "The Multitrait-Multirater Approach to Measuring Managerial Job Performance." *Journal of Applied Psychology*, October 1967, *51*, 5, 369–380.

Lawler, Edward E. & Lyman W. Porter. "The Effect of Performance on Job Satisfaction." *Industrial Relations*, October 1967, *7*, 1, 20–28.

Lawrence, Paul R. & Jay Lorsch. *Organization and Environment*. Boston: Harvard University Press, 1967.

Lazarsfeld, Paul F. & Wagner Thielens, Jr. *The Academic Mind*. Glencoe, IL: The Free Press, 1958.

Lenning, Oscar T., Yong S. Lee, Sidney S. Micek, & Allen L. Service. *A Structure for the Outcomes of Postsecondary Education*. Boulder, CO: National Center for Higher Education Management Systems, 1977.

Leslie, David W. "Legitimizing University Governance: Theory and Practice." *Higher Education*, May 1975, *4*, 2, 233–246.

Lewin, Arie Y. & John W. Minton. "Determining Organizational Effectiveness." *Management Science*, May 1986, *32*, 5, 514–538.

Light, Donald W., Jr. "The Academic Career." *Dialogue*, 1973, *6*, 3, 34–41.

Light, Donald W., Jr., L. R. Mardsen, & T. C. Cori. *The Impact of the Academic Revolution on Faculty Careers*. ERIC/AAHE Research Reports, No. 10. Washington, DC: American Association for Higher Education, 1973.

Lincoln, James R., Mitsuyo Hanada, & Jon Olson. "Cultural Orientations and Individual Reactions to Organizations — A Study of Employees of Japanese-Owned Firms." *Administrative Science Quarterly*, March 1981, *26*, 1, 93–115.

Lindblom, Charles E. "The Science of Muddling Through." *Public Administration Review*, Spring 1959, *19*, 2, 79–88.

Lindquist, John D. & Robert T. Blackburn. "Middlegrove: The Locus of Campus Power at a State University." *AAUP Bulletin*, Winter 1974, *60*, 4, 367–378.

Lodahl, Thomas M., Janice Beyer, & Gerald Gordon. "The Structure of Scientific Fields and the Functioning of University Graduate Departments." *American Sociological Review*, February 1972, *37*, 1, 57–72.

Lorsch, Jay W. & Stephen A. Allen III. *Managing Diversity and Interdependence*. Boston: Harvard University, Graduate School of Business Administration, 1973.

Lortie, Dan C. *School Teacher*. Chicago: University of Chicago Press, 1975.

Louis, Meryl Reis. "An Investigator's Guide to Workplace Culture," in Peter Frost et al., *Organizational Culture*. Beverly Hills: Sage Publications, 1985.

Lunsford, Terry F. "Authority and Ideology in the Administered University," in Carlos E. Kruytbosch & Sheldon L. Messinger (eds.), *The State of the University*. Beverly Hills: Sage Publications, 1963.

Lyden, Freemont James. "Using Parsons' Functional Analysis in the Study of Public Organizations." *Administrative Science Quarterly*, March 1975, *20*, 1, 59–70.

McKelvey, Bill. "Toward More Comprehensive Organization Design Objectives," in Ralph H. Kilmann, Louis R. Pondy, & Dennis P. Slevin (eds.), *The Management of Organization Design*. Volume 1. New York: Elsevier North-Holland, 1976, 27–46.

MacMillan, Ian C. *Strategy Formulation: Political Concepts*. St. Paul: West Publishing Co., 1978.

Malott, Richard, Mary Tillema, & Sigrid Glenn. *Behavior Analysis*. Michigan: Behaviordelia, Inc., 1978.

Mannheim, Karl. *Man and Society in an Age of Reconstruction.* New York: Harcourt Brace Jovanovich, 1940.

Mann, Richard D. & Associates. *The College Classroom.* New York: John Wiley & Sons, 1970.

March, James G. "The Technology of Foolishness," in James G. March & Johan P. Olsen (eds.), *Ambiguity and Choice in Organizations.* Bergen, Norway: Universitets Forlaget, 1976, 69–81.

March, James G. & Johan P. Olsen. *Ambiguity and Choice in Organizations.* Bergen, Norway: Universitets Forlaget, 1976.

March, James G. & Herbert A. Simon. *Organizations.* New York: John Wiley & Sons, 1958.

Masland, Andrew T. "Organizational Culture in the Study of Higher Education." *Review of Higher Education,* Winter 1985, *8,* 2, 157–168.

Meyer, John W. & Brian Rowan. "Institutionalized Organizations: Structure as Myth and Ceremony." *American Journal of Sociology,* 1977, *83,* 340–363.

Meyer, Marshall W. "'Bureaucratic' Versus 'Profit' Organization." *Research in Organizational Behavior,* 1982, *4,* 89–126.

Miles, Raymond E. "Human Relations or Human Resources." *Harvard Business Review,* July–August 1965, *43,* 4, 148–163.

Miles, Raymond E. "Governance of Organizations: Leader–Led Roles," in George W. England, Anant R. Negandhi, & Bernhard Wilpert (eds.), *The Functioning of Complex Organizations.* Cambridge, MA: Oelgeschlager, Gunn and Hain, Publishers, Inc., 1981, 173–202.

Miles, Raymond E. & C. Snow. *Organization Strategy, Structure and Process.* New York: McGraw Hill, 1978.

Miles, Robert H. *Macro Organizational Behavior.* Santa Monica: Goodyear Publishing Company, 1980.

Miller, G. E. Galanter & K. Pribram. *Plans and the Structure of Behavior.* New York: Holt, 1960.

Millett, John D. *The Academic Community.* New York: McGraw Hill, 1962.

Millett, John D. *New Structures of Campus Power.* San Francisco: Jossey-Bass Publishers, 1978.

Mintzberg, Henry. *The Structure of Organizations.* Englewood Cliffs, NJ: Prentice-Hall, 1979.

Mintzberg, Henry. *Power In and Around Organizations.* Englewood Cliffs, NJ: Prentice-Hall, 1983a.

Mintzberg, Henry. *Structure in Fives, Designing Effective Organizations.* Englewood Cliffs, NJ: Prentice-Hall, 1983b.

Mintzberg, Henry. "Power and Organizational Life Cycles." *Academy of Management Review,* April 1984, *9,* 2, 207–224.

Mintzberg, Henry, Durn Raisinghani, & Andre Theoret. "The Structure of Unstructured Decision Process." *Administrative Science Quarterly,* June 1976, *21,* 2, 246–275.

Mitroff, Ian & Ralph R. Kilmann. *Methodological Approaches to the Social Sciences.* San Francisco: Jossey-Bass Publishers, 1978.

Mitroff, Ian & Ralph R. Kilmann. "The Stories Managers Tell: A New Tool for Organizational Problem Solving." *Management Review,* July 1975, *64,* 7, 18–28.

Mohr, Lawrence B. *Explaining Organizational Behavior.* San Francisco: Jossey-Bass Publishers, 1982.

Mortimer, Kenneth P. & T. R. McConnell. *Sharing Authority Effectively*. San Francisco: Jossey-Bass Publishers, 1978.

Muchinsky, Paul M. & Paula C. Morrow. "The Applicability of Middle Range Theories to the Study of Organizational Effectiveness," in Craig C. Pinder & Larry F. Moore (eds.), *Middle Range Theory and the Study of Organizations*. Boston: Martinus Nijhoff Publishing, 1980, 304–314.

Nadler, David A. *Feedback and Organization Development: Using Data-Based Methods*. Reading, MA: Addison-Wesley, 1977.

Nadler, David A., Richard Hackman, & Edward E. Lawler III. *Managing Organizational Behavior*. Boston: Little Brown, 1979.

Nadler, David A. & Michael L. Tushman. "A Diagnostic Model for Organizational Behavior," in J. Richard Hackman, Edward E. Lawler III, & Lyman W. Porter (eds.), *Perspectives on Behavior in Organizations*. New York: McGraw-Hill, 1977, 85–97.

Nadler, David A. & Michael L. Tushman. "Information Processing as an Integrating Concept in Organization Design." *Academy of Management Review*, December 1978, *3*, 4, 613–624.

National Academy of Sciences. *Mobility of Ph.D's Before and After the Doctorate*. Washington, DC: National Academy of Sciences, 1971.

Neumann, L. & Y. Neumann. "Faculty Perceptions of Deans and Department Chairpersons' Management Functions." *Higher Education*, 1983, *12*, 2, 205–214.

Neumann, Yoram. "Predicting Faculty Job Satisfaction in University Departments." *Research in Higher Education*, 1978, *9*, 3, 261–276.

Nord, Walter R. "Developments in the Study of Power," in Walter R. Nord (ed.), *Concepts and Controversy in Organizational Behavior*, 2nd Ed. Santa Monica: Goodyear Publishing Company, 1976, 538–543.

Ouchi, William G. "The Relationship Between Organizational Structure and Organizational Control." *Administrative Science Quarterly*, March 1977, *22*, 1, 95–113.

Ouchi, William G. "The Transmission of Control Through Organizational Hierarchy." *Academy of Management Journal*, 1978, *21*, 2, 173–192.

Ouchi, William G. *Theory Z: How American Business Can Meet the Japanese Challenge*. Reading, MA: Addison-Wesley Publishing Co., 1981.

Ouchi, William G. & Mary Ann Maguire. "Organizational Control: Two Functions." *Administrative Science Quarterly*, December 1975, *20*, 4, 559–569.

Parsons, Talcott. *The Social System*. Glencoe, IL: The Free Press, 1951.

Parsons, Talcott. "The Theory of Symbolism in Relation to Action," in Talcott Parsons, Robert F. Bales, & Edward A Shils, *Working Papers in the Theory of Action*. New York: The Free Press, 1953.

Parsons, Talcott. "General Theory in Sociology," in Robert K. Merton, Leonard Broom, & Leonard S. Cottrell, Jr. (eds.), *Sociology Today*. New York: Basic Books, 1959.

Parsons, Talcott. "Pattern Variables Revisited: A Response to Robert Dubin." *American Sociological Review*, August 1960a, *25*, 4, 467–483.

Parsons, Talcott. *Structure and Process in Modern Societies*. New York: The Free Press, 1960b.

Parsons, Talcott. "The Strange Case of Academic Organization." *Journal of Higher Education*, June 1971, *47*, 6, 486–495.

Parsons, Talcott & Gerald M. Platt. *The American Academic Profession: A Pilot Study*. Cambridge, MA: Harvard University Press, 1968.

Parsons, Talcott & Gerald M. Platt. *The American University*. Cambridge, MA: Harvard University Press, 1973.

Parsons, Talcott, Robert F. Bales, & Edward A. Shils. "Phase Movement in Relation to Motivation," in *Working Papers in the Theory of Action*. New York: The Free Press, 1953.

Paxton, Dan R. & Darwin L. Thomas. "College Presidents' Role Performance and Faculty Satisfaction." *Research in Higher Education*, 1977, *7*, 4, 341–353.

Payne, R. L. "The Influence of Structure at Organizational and Group Levels." *Administrative Science Quarterly*, September 1971, *16*, 1, 61–73.

Perrow, Charles. *Organizational Analysis: A Sociological View*. Belmont, CA: Wadsworth Publishing Company, Inc., 1970.

Perrow, Charles. *Complex Organizations: A Critical Essay*. Glenview, IL: Scott Foresman, 1972.

Perrow, Charles. "The Short and Glorious History of Organizational Theory." *Organizational Dynamics*, Summer 1973, *2*, 1, 2–15.

Peters, Diane S. "Temporal Perceptions and University Faculty." *Research in Higher Education*, 1979, *11*, 2, 179–186.

Pettigrew, Andrew M. *The Politics of Organizational Decision-Making*. London: Tavistock, 1973.

Pfeffer, Jeffrey. "Power and Resource Allocation in Organizations," in Barry M. Staw & Gerald R. Salancik (eds.), *New Directions in Organizational Behavior*. Chicago: St. Clair Press, 1977, 235–266.

Pfeffer, Jeffrey. *Organizational Design*. Arlington Heights: IL: HM Publishing Corporation, 1978.

Pfeffer, Jeffrey. "The Micropolitics of Organizations," in Marshall W. Meyer and Associates, *Environments and Organizations*. San Francisco: Jossey-Bass Publishers, 1980.

Pfeffer, Jeffrey. *Power in Organizations*. Marshfield, MA: Pitman Publishing, 1981.

Pfeffer, Jeffrey. *Organizations and Organization Theory*. Boston: Pitman Publishing Co., 1982.

Pfeffer, Jeffrey & John Lawler. "Effects of Job Alternatives, Extrinsic Rewards, and Behavioral Commitment on Attitude Toward the Organization: A Field Test of the Insufficient Justification Paradigm." *Administrative Science Quarterly*, March 1980, *25*, 1, 38–56.

Pfeffer, Jeffrey & Gerald R. Salancik. "Organizational Decision Making as a Political Process: The Case of a University Budget." *Administrative Science Quarterly*, June 1974, *19*, 2, 135–151.

Pfeffer, Jeffrey, Gerald R. Salancik, & H. Leblebici. "The Effect of Uncertainty on the Use of Influence in Organizational Decision-Making." *Administrative Science Quarterly*, June 1976, *21*, 2, 227–245.

Platt, Gerald M. & Talcott Parsons. "Decision-Making in the Academic System, Influence and Power Exchange," in Carlos E. Kruytbosch & Sheldon L. Messinger (eds.), *The State of the University: Authority and Change*. Beverly Hills: Sage Publications, 1968, 133–178.

Platt, Gerald M., Talcott Parsons, & Rita Kirstein. "Faculty Teaching Goals, 1968–1973." *Social Problems*, December 1976, *24*, 2, 298–306.

Porter, Lyman W., Robert W. Allen, & Harold L. Angle. "The Politics of Upward Influence in Organizations," in Robert W. Allen & Lyman W. Porter (eds.), *Organizational Influence Processes*. Glenview, IL: Scott, Foresman, 1983, 402–422.

Powers, David R. & Mary F. Powers. *Making Participatory Management Work*. San Francisco: Jossey-Bass Publishers, 1983.

Pugh, D. S., D. J. Hickson, & C. R. Hinings. "An Empirical Taxonomy of Structures of Work Organizations." *Administrative Science Quarterly*, March 1969, *14*, 1, 115–126.

Ranson, Stewart, Bob Hinings, & Royston Greenwood. "The Structuring of Organizational Structures." *Administrative Science Quarterly*, March 1980, *25*, 1, 1–17.

Reid, John Y. "Politics and Quality in Administrator Evaluation." *Research in Higher Education*, 1982, *16*, 1, 27–40.

Rich, Harvey E. & Pamela M. Jolicoer. "Faculty Role Perceptions and Preferences in the Seventies." *Sociology of Work and Occupations*, November 1978, *5*, 4, 423–445.

Riesman, David. *Constraint and Variety in American Education*. Lincoln, NE: University of Nebraska Press, 1956.

Robbins, Stephen P. "The Theory Z Organization from a Power-Control Perspective." *California Management Review*, January 1983, *25*, 2, 67–75.

Robertson, D. B. (ed.). *Power and Empowerment in Higher Education*. Lexington, KY: The University Press of Kentucky, 1978.

Ronen, Simcha. "Personal Values: A Basis for Work Motivational Set and Work Attitude." *Organizational Behavior and Human Performance*. February 1978, *21*, 1, 80–107.

Rosencrance, Francis C. *The American College and Its Teachers*. New York: The Macmillan Co., 1962.

Rosner, Menachem. "Participatory Political and Organizational Democracy and the Experience of the Israeli Kibbutz," in Colin Crouch & Frank A. Heller (eds.), *Organizational Democracy and Political Processes*. Volume 1, International Yearbook of Organizational Democracy. New York: John Wiley & Sons, 1983, 455–482.

Rossi, Peter H. & Richard A. Berk. "Varieties of Normative Consensus." *American Sociological Review*, June 1985, *50*, 333–347.

Rothschild-Whitt, Joyce. "The Collectivist Organization: An Alternative to Rational-Bureaucratic Models." *American Sociological Review*, August 1979, *44*, 509–527.

Rubin, Irene S. "Retrenchment, Loose Structure and Adaptability in the University." *Sociology of Education*, October 1979, *53*, 4, 211–222.

Russell, Kevin J. "Variations in Orientation to Work and Job Satisfaction." *Sociology of Work and Occupations*, November 1975, *2*, 4.

Ryan, Doris W. "Deans as Individuals-in-Organizations," in Daniel E. Griffiths & Donald J. McCarty (eds.), *The Dilemma of the Deanship*. Danville, IL: The Interstate Printers and Publishers, Inc., 1980, 133–173.

Ryans, David G. "An Analysis and Comparison of Certain Techniques for Weighting Criterion Data." *Educational and Psychological Measurement*, Autumn 1954, *14*, 3, 449–458.

Salaman, Graeme. "Organizations as Constructors of Social Reality (II)," in Graeme Salaman & Kenneth Thompson (eds.), *Control and Ideology in Organizations*. Cambridge, MA: The MIT Press, 1980, 237–258.

Salancik, Gerald R. & Jeffrey Pfeffer. "Who Gets Power—and How They Hold on to It: A Strategic-Contingency Model of Power." *Organizational Dynamics*, Winter 1977, *5*, 1, 2–21.

Satow, R. L. "Value-Rational Authority and Professional Organizations: Weber's Missing Type." *Administrative Science Quarterly*, December 1975, *20*, 4, 526–531.

Schein, Edgar H. "Coming to a New Awareness of Organizational Culture." *Sloan Management Review*, Winter 1984, *25*, 2, 3-16.

Schein, Edgar H. *Organizational Culture and Leadership*. San Francisco: Jossey-Bass Publishers, 1985.

Schram, Wilbur. "Information Theory and Mass Communication." *Journalism Quarterly*, Spring 1955, *32*, 2, 131-146.

Schriesheim, Janet, Mary Ann Von Glinow, & Steven Kerr. "Professionals in Bureaucracies: A Structural Alternative," in Paul C. Nystrom & William H. Starbuck (eds.), *Prescriptive Models of Organizations*. New York: Elsevier Science Publishing Co., Inc., TIMS Studies in the Management Sciences, 1977, *5*, 55-69.

Scott, William G., Terence R. Mitchell, & Philip H. Birnbaum. "Organizational Governance," in *Organizational Theory: A Structural and Behavioral Analysis*, 4th Ed. Homewood, IL: Richard D. Irwin, Inc., 1981.

Scott, William G., Terence R. Mitchell, & Newman S. Peary. "Organizational Governance," in Paul C. Nystrom & William H. Starbuck (eds.), *Handbook of Organizational Design*, Volume 2. New York: Oxford University Press, 1981, 135-151.

Scott, W. Richard. "Effectiveness of Organizational Effectiveness Studies," in Paul S. Goodman & Johannes Pennings (eds.), *New Perspectives on Organizational Effectiveness*. San Francisco: Jossey-Bass Publishers, 1977, 63-95.

Scott, W. Richard. *Organizations*. Englewood Cliffs, NJ: Prentice-Hall, 1981.

Seashore, Stanley E. "Defining and Measuring the Quality of Working Life," in Louis E. Davis, Albert B. Cherns, & Associates, *The Quality of Working Life*, Volume 1. New York: The Free Press, 1975, 105-118.

Selznick, Philip. *Leadership in Administration*. New York: Harper & Row Publishers, 1957.

Sheehy, Gail. *Passages: Predictable Crises of Adult Life*. New York: Dutton, 1976.

Simon, Herbert A. *Administrative Behavior*, 2nd Ed. New York: The Free Press, 1957.

Smart, John C. & Charles F. Elton. "Goal Orientations of Academic Departments." *Journal of Applied Psychology*, 1975, *60*, 580-588.

Smart, John C. & Gerald W. McLaughlin. "Reward Structures in Academic Disciplines." *Research in Higher Education*, 1978, *8*, 1, 67-82

Smelser, Neil J. "Epilogue," in Talcott Parsons & Gerald M. Platt, *The American University*. Cambridge, MA: Harvard University Press, 1973.

Smircich, Linda. "Concepts of Culture and Organizational Analysis." *Administrative Science Quarterly*, September 1983, *28*, 3, 339-358.

Spray, S. L. (ed.). *Organizational Effectiveness: Theory, Research and Application*. Kent, OH: Kent State University Press, 1976.

Sproul, Lee S. "Beliefs in Organizations," in Paul C. Nystrom & William H. Starbuck (eds.), *Handbook of Organizational Design*, Volume 2. New York: Oxford University Press, 1981, 203-224.

Staw, Barry M. "The Self-Perception of Motivation," in Barry M. Staw (ed.), *Intrinsic and Extrinsic Motivation*. Morristown, NJ: General Learning Press, 1976.

Staw, Barry M. "Motivation in Organizations: Toward Synthesis and Redirection," in Barry M. Staw & Gerald R. Salancik (eds.), *New Directions in Organizational Behavior*. Chicago: St. Clair Press, 1977.

Staw, Barry M. "Rationality and Justification in Organizational Life," in Barry M. Staw & Larry L. Cummings (eds.), *Research in Organizational Behavior*, Volume 2. Greenwich, CT: JAI Press, 1980, 45-80.

Steele, F. & S. Jenks. *The Feel of the Workplace: Understanding and Improving Organizational Climate.* Reading, MA: Addison-Wesley, 1977.

Steers, Richard M. "Problems in the Measurement of Organizational Effectiveness." *Administrative Science Quarterly*, December 1975, *20*, 4, 546–558.

Steers, Richard M. *Organizational Effectiveness, A Behavioral View.* Santa Monica: Goodyear Publishing Company, 1977.

Stein, Barry A. & Rosabeth Moss Kanter. "Building the Parallel Organization: Creating Mechanisms for Permanent Quality of Work Life." *The Journal of Applied Behavioral Science*, July/August/September 1980, *16*, 3, 371–388.

Strauss, Anselm. *Negotiations.* San Francisco: Jossey-Bass Publishers, 1978.

Szilagyi, Andrew D., Jr. & David M. Schweiger. "Matching Managers to Strategies: A Review and Suggested Framework." *Academy of Management Review*, 1984, *9*, 4, 626–637.

Thomas, Kenneth. "Conflict and Conflict Management," in Marvin E. Dunnette (ed.), *Handbook of Industrial and Organizational Psychology.* Chicago: Rand McNally College Publishing Company, 1976, 889–936.

Thompson, James D. *Organizations in Action.* New York: McGraw Book Company, 1967.

Thompson, James D. & Arthur Tuden. *Comparative Studies in Administration.* Pittsburgh: University of Pittsburgh Press, 1959.

Thompson, James D., Robert W. Hawkes, & Robert W. Avery. "Truth Strategies and University Organization." *Educational Administration Quarterly*, Spring 1969, *5*, 2, 4–25.

Thompson, Kenneth R. & Fred Luthans. "A Behavioral Interpretation of Power," in Robert W. Allen & Lyman W. Porter (eds.), *Organizational Influence Processes.* Glenview, IL: Scott Foresman, 1983, 72–86.

Tichy, Noel M., Michael L. Tushman, & Charles Fombrun. "Network Analysis in Organizations," in Edward E. Lawler III, David A. Nadler, & Cortlandt Camman (eds.), *Organizational Assessment.* New York: John Wiley & Sons, 1980, 372–398.

Tonn, Joan C. "Political Behavior in Higher Education Budgeting." *Journal of Higher Education*, 1978, *49*, 6, 575–587.

Trow, Martin A. (ed.). *Teachers and Students.* New York: McGraw-Hill, 1975.

Trow, Martin A. & Oliver Fulton. "Research Activity in American Higher Education," in Martin A. Trow (ed.), *Teachers and Students.* New York: McGraw-Hill, 1975, 39–83.

Tushman, Michael L. "Work Characteristics and Subunit Communication Structure: A Contingency Analysis." *Administrative Science Quarterly*, March 1979, *24*, 1, 82–98.

Tushman, Michael L. & David A. Nadler. "Information Processing as an Integrating Concept in Organizational Design." *Academy of Management Review*, 1978, 613–624.

Tushman, Michael L. & David A. Nadler. "A Model for Diagnosing Organizational Behavior." *Organizational Dynamics*, 1980, *9*, 2, 35–51.

Tyler, William B. "Measuring Organizational Specialization: The Concept of Role Variety." *Administrative Science Quarterly*, September 1973, *18*, 3, 383–392.

Van de Ven, Andrew H. & Andre L. Delbecq. "A Task Contingent Model of Workunit Structure." *Administrative Science Quarterly*, June 1974, *19*, 2, 183–197.

Van de Ven, Andrew H., Andre L. Delbecq, & Richard Koenig, Jr. "Determinants of Coordinating Modes Within Organizations." *American Sociological Review*, April 1976, *41*, 2, 322–338.

Van de Ven, Andrew H. & Robert Drazin. "The Concept of Fit in Contingency Theory," in Barry M. Staw & Larry L. Cummings (eds.), *Research in Organizational Behavior*, Volume 7. Greenwich, CT: JAI Press, 1985, 333–365.

Van Maanen, John & Stephen R. Barley. "Cultural Organization, Fragments of a Theory," in Peter J. Frost, Larry F. Moore, Meryl Reis Louis, Graig C. Lundberg, & Joanne Martin (eds.), *Organizational Culture*. Beverly Hills: Sage Publications, 1985, 31–53.

Van Sell, Mary, Arthur P. Brief, & Randall S. Schuler. "Role Conflict and Role Ambiguity: Integration of the Literature and Directions for Future Research." *Human Relations*, January 1981, *34*, 1, 43–67.

Varela, Jacob A. "The Design of Persuasions," in *Psychological Solutions to Social Problems: An Introduction to Social Technology*. New York: Academic Press, 1971, 84–110.

Vroom, Victor H. "Leaders and Leadership in Academe," in James L. Bess (ed.), *College and University Organization: Insights from the Behavioral Sciences*. New York: New York University Press, 1984, 129–148.

Vroom, Victor H. *Work and Motivation*. New York: John Wiley & Sons, 1964.

Vroom, Victor H. & Philip W. Yetton. *Leadership and Decision-Making*. Pittsburgh: University of Pittsburgh Press, 1973.

Weber, Max. *The Theory of Social and Economic Organization* (Talcott Parsons, ed.; A. M. Henderson & Talcott Parsons, trans.). New York: Free Press, 1947.

Weick, Karl E. *The Social Psychology of Organizing*. Reading, MA: Addison-Wesley, 1969.

Weick, Karl E. "Educational Organizations as Loosely Coupled Systems." *Administrative Science Quarterly*, March 1976, *21*, 1, 1–19.

Weick, Karl E. "The Spines of Leaders," in M. W. McCall, Jr. & M. M. Lombardo (eds.), *Leadership: Where Else Can We Go?* Durham, NC: Duke University Press, 1978.

Weick, Karl E. *The Social Psychology of Organizing*, 2d Ed. Reading, MA: Addison-Wesley, 1979.

Weick, Karl E. "Contradictions in a Community of Scholars: the Cohesion–Accuracy Tradeoff," in James L. Bess (ed.), *College and University Organization: Insights from the Behavioral Sciences*. New York: New York University Press, 1984, 15–30.

Wilkins, Alan L. & William G. Ouchi. "Efficient Cultures: Exploring the Relationship Between Culture and Organizational Performance." *Administrative Science Quarterly*, September 1983, *28*, 3, 468–481.

Williamson, O. E. "Markets and Hierarchies: Some Elementary Considerations." *American Economic Review*, 1973, *63*, 316–325.

Willie, John R. & John E. Stecklein. "A Three Decade Comparison of College Faculty Characteristics, Satisfactions, Activities and Attitudes." *Research in Higher Education*, 1982, *16*, 81–93.

Wilmott, Hugh. "What Does the Concept of 'Organizational Structure' Mean? A Clarification of Its Use." Paper presented at the Conference on Critical Perspectives in Organizations, Baruch College, New York, September 1985.

Wilson, Logan. *The Academic Man*. New York: Oxford University Press, 1942.

Woodward, Joan. *Industrial Organization*. London: Oxford University Press, 1965.

Yuchtman, Ephraim & Stanley E. Seasnore. "A System Resource Approach to

Organizational Effectiveness." *American Sociological Review*, December 1967, *32*, 6, 891–903.

Zaleznik, Abraham. "Power and Politics in Organizational Life." *Harvard Business Review*, May–June 1970, *48*, 3, 47–60.

Zand, Dale E. "Trust and Managerial Problem Solving." *Administrative Science Quarterly*, June 1972, *17*, 2, 229–239.

Zand, Dale E. "Collateral Organization: A New Change Strategy." *Journal of Applied Behavioral Science*, 1974, *10*, 1, 63–89.

Zand, Dale E. *Information, Organization, and Power*. New York: McGraw-Hill, 1981, 57-88.

Zander, Alvin, Arthur R. Cohen, & Ezra Stotland. "Power and the Relations Among Professions," in Dorwin Cartwright (ed.), *Studies in Social Power*. Ann Arbor: University of Michigan, Institute for Social Research, 1959, 15–34.

Zucker, Lynne G. "Production of Trust: Institutional Sources of Economic Structures, 1840–1920," in Barry M. Staw & Larry L. Cummings (eds.), *Research in Organizational Behavior*, Volume 8. Greenwich, CT: JAI Press, 1986, 53–111.

INDEX

ABOUT THE AUTHOR

James L. Bess was born in 1934 in Forest Hills, New York. He was graduated from Cornell University in 1956, spent two years as a guided-missile officer in the Army, earned an M.B.A. from Harvard, an M.A. from New York University, and a Ph.D. from the University of California, Berkeley. After working in financial management for a large New York publisher, he served in various administrative posts in higher education. In 1976 he joined the faculty at Teachers College, Columbia University, then moved in 1980 to New York University, where he now teaches. Dr. Bess has written or edited three other books besides this one and has published numerous articles in professional journals. In 1986–87, with the partial aid of a Fulbright award, he spent a year on sabbatical in Japan conducting research on the management of scientific research and development laboratories in universities, corporations, and government institutes. Similar studies are planned for England and the United States. Dr. Bess lives with his wife, a professional fiber artist, and their two children in New York City and in a small summer cottage in northwest Connecticut.